Corporate Governance

Corporate Governance

Responsibilities, Risks and Remuneration

Edited by
Kevin Keasey and Mike Wright

JOHN WILEY & SONS

Chichester • New York • Weinheim • Brisbane • Singapore • Toronto

Other Wiley Editorial Offices

John Wiley & Sons, Inc., 605 Third Avenue,
New York, NY 10158-0012, USA

VCH Verlagsgesellschaft mbH Pappelallee 3,
D–69469 Weinheim, Germany

Jacaranda Wiley Ltd, 33 Park Road, Milton,
Queensland 4064, Australia

John Wiley & Sons (Canada) Ltd, 22 Worcester Road,
Rexdale, Ontario M9W 1L1, Canada

John Wiley & Sons (Asia) Pte Ltd, 2 Clementi Loop #02-01,
Jin Xing Distripark, Singapore 129809

Library of Congress Cataloging-in-Publication Data

Corporate governance : responsibilities, risks, and remuneration /
edited by Kevin Keasey and Mike Wright.
    p.   cm.
  Includes bibliographical references and index.
  ISBN 0–471–97021–2
    1. Corporate governance. I. Keasey, Kevin. II. Wright, Mike,
1952–.
HD2741.C777   1997
658.4—DC20   96–34874
                                                         CIP

British Library Cataloguing in Publication Data

A catalogue record for this book is available from the British Library

ISBN 0-471-97021-2

Typeset in 11/13pt Times from the author's disks by Keytec Typesetting Ltd, Bridport, Dorset
Printed and bound in Great Britain by Biddles Ltd, Guildford and King's Lynn
This book is printed on acid-free paper responsibly manufactured from sustainable forestation,
for which at least two trees are planted for each one used for paper production.

Contents

List of Contributors

Paul Collier is a senior lecturer in accounting, in the Department of Economics, University of Exeter, Exeter EX4 4RJ.

Mahmoud Ezzamel is a Professor of Accounting, the Department of Accounting and Finance, University of Manchester, Manchester M13 9PL.

Kevin Keasey is the Leeds Permanent Building Society Professor of Financial Services and Director of the Centre for Financial Services, University of Leeds, Leeds LS2 9JT.

Christine Mallin is Professor of Finance, Nottingham Business School, Nottingham Trent University, Nottingham NG1 4BU.

Roger Mills is Professor of Accounting Studies, Henley Management College, Henley on Thames, Oxon RG9 3AU.

Helen Short is lecturer in Accounting and Finance, The School of Business and Economic Studies, University of Leeds, Leeds LS2 9JT.

Robert Watson is Professor of Finance and Accounting, The School of Business and Economic Studies, University of Leeds, Leeds LS2 9JT.

Mike Wright is Professor of Financial Studies and Director of the Centre for Management Buy-out Research, University of Nottingham, Nottingham NG7 2RD.

Preface

This text is based upon a research programme into financial aspects of corporate governance funded by the Research Board of the Institute of Chartered Accountants in England and Wales. The points of view expressed in the individual chapters are those of the individual authors and are not necessarily those of the Institute, its Research Board (or the organisations with which the authors are associated).

Introduction
Corporate Governance, Accountability and Enterprise

KEVIN KEASEY and MIKE WRIGHT

INTRODUCTION

Although corporate governance has been a long-standing issue, the debate was given fresh impetus, in the UK at least, by a number of well-publicised corporate problems in the late 1980s. These involved creative accounting, spectacular business failures, the apparent ease of unscrupulous directors in expropriating other stakeholders' funds, the limited role of auditors, the claimed weak link between executive compensation and company performance, and the roles played by the market for corporate control and institutional investors in generating apparently excessive short-term perspectives to the detriment of general economic performance. The report of the Cadbury Committee (1992) was a response to these concerns. In particular, the Committee's terms of reference required it to examine financial aspects of corporate governance.

This volume presents the results of a number of studies carried out under the auspices of the corporate governance initiative of the Research Board of the ICAEW. These studies focused on key aspects of the recommendations of the Cadbury Committee, notably in respect of the roles of institutional investors, audit committees, executive remuneration and internal controls.

The Cadbury Committee's terms of reference were restricted to issues of accountability. As a result there has been considerable focus on this subset of the more general issue of corporate governance. As the corporate governance debate has developed, however, the balance between accountability and enterprise has emerged as a key issue. Indeed, it is interesting to observe that the parallel corporate governance debate in the US has placed more emphasis on enhancing performance.

This introductory chapter provides an overview of both the key aspects of the corporate governance debate and the contents of the volume. It is structured as follows. The next section outlines a corporate governance framework and relates the main recommendations of the Cadbury Committee to it. The issues addressed in the main body of the volume are then reviewed: executive remuneration, audit committees, internal controls and institutional investors. In the light of the increasing attention given to the need to balance accountability and enterprise for the achievement of effective governance, the penultimate section discusses recent developments in this area. The final section provides some conclusions and pointers for further research.

A FRAMEWORK OF CORPORATE GOVERNANCE AND CADBURY

There is considerable debate about what actually constitutes corporate governance but its key elements concern the enhancement of corporate performance via the supervision, or monitoring, of management performance and ensuring the accountability of management to shareholders and other stakeholders. These aspects of governance and accountability are closely interrelated and introduce both efficiency and stewardship dimensions to corporate governance. Stewardship emphasises issues concerning, for example, the misappropriation of funds by non-owner managers. Equally important, however, is the issue of how the structure and process of governance motivates entrepreneurial activities which increase the wealth of the business. Corporate entrepreneurship concerns the reallocation of economic resources in new combinations and may involve both innovations as well as major corporate restructuring (Guth and Ginsberg, 1990). Good corporate governance is, thus, as much concerned with correctly motivating managerial behaviour towards improving the business, as directly controlling the behaviour of managers. For example, executive remuneration, especially if it involves increasing the ownership

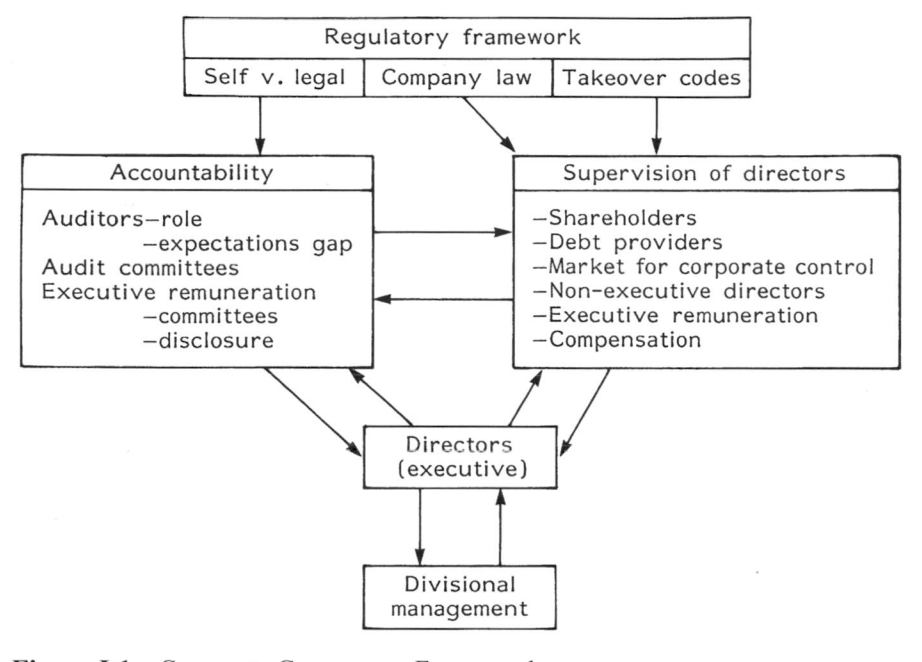

Figure I.1 Corporate Governance Framework

stake of directors may be one means of motivating good behaviour; although, even here, the evidence is somewhat mixed (for example, see Short and Keasey, 1996a). Not surprisingly, given the differing nature of the interests involved, considerable problems arise in devising appropriate remuneration contracts that both motivate managers and are in the best interests of shareholders. A further aspect of accountability is, therefore, to monitor and disclose such issues.

The need for the supervision and accountability of directors arises because of the so-called divorce between ownership and control in large enterprises with diffuse ownership (Hart, 1995). Supervision may take various forms ranging from systems where shareholders are 'outsiders' with little direct incentive to monitor management and where emphasis is placed on the role of the takeover mechanism to discipline underperforming managers, to systems where shareholders are 'insiders' with very close involvement in the management of the enterprise. Issues concerning the appropriate supervisory system also extend below the top-tier level to the problems of dealing with divisional managers.

Third parties have a key role to play in ensuring the accountability of directors and management, especially auditors and non-executive directors. This in turn raises the question of what their roles are expected to be and the difficulties in carrying them out. The existence of a gap between what auditors are legally required to do and what they are expected to do by society in general is one manifestation of the problem (Humphry, Moizer and Turley, 1993). Nonetheless, it has to be noted that the supervision and accountability aspects of corporate governance take place within a wider regulatory framework which regulates relationships with external third party contractors and this forms a further major part of the present framework and includes elements of self-regulation and statutory rules (Whittington, 1993).

The proposals of the Cadbury Committee focused primarily on the accountability aspects of corporate governance portrayed in Figure I.1. They relied largely upon improved information to shareholders, continued self-regulation and a strengthening of auditor independence. The principal recommendations of the Cadbury Committee, encapsulated in a Code of Best Practice, addressed here aimed to improve corporate governance in the following ways.

* All listed companies should establish an audit committee comprising at least three non-executive directors. The primary brief of audit committees is to review the financial statements and the findings of the external auditors. They can thus be seen as an attempt specifically to designate responsibility for accounting-related matters, to provide a non-confrontational reporting structure for insiders and to supervise relations with the external auditor in an independent manner.

⤳ There should be a remuneration committee which determines executives' pay, directors should not be appointed for more than three years without shareholders' approval, the roles of chairman and chief executive officer should be separated, the emoluments of the chairman and highest-paid UK director should be disclosed and the computation of performance-related pay fully explained. In an important recommendation concerning disclosure, information should be provided in a form which differentiates between salary and performance-related components and the basis for determining the latter should be explained. To emphasise the importance of independent directors in setting executive directors' remuneration, a remuneration committee should be established made up wholly or mainly of non-executive directors. In order to address accountability issues relating to internal links between parents and subsidiaries, recommendations were also made concerning the need to produce statements on the effectiveness of internal financial control and the business as a going concern.

The following sections review the major issues and findings from the main chapters of this book relating to these aspects of corporate account-ability.

EXECUTIVE REMUNERATION

Executive remuneration has become one of the most controversial aspects of the current corporate governance debate. The Cadbury recommenda-tions in respect of remuneration committees, outlined earlier, were intended to strengthen the link between executive pay and performance. However, public concerns about the level and nature of executive re-muneration subsequently led to recommendations in respect of this issue by the Greenbury Committee (subsequently implemented by the Stock Exchange Listing Rules).

In their analysis in Chapter 2 of a sample of 199 companies from *The Times Top 1000* listed firms, Mahmoud Ezzamel and Robert Watson find that changes in executive pay are more closely related to external market comparisons of pay levels than to changes in either profits or shareholder wealth. They also point to a marked asymmetry in treatment between those executives who appeared to be, relative to market comparison pay levels, under- and overpaid. Executives who were relatively underpaid in the previous period were found to experience a large and highly signifi-cant increase in their pay in the following year. There was, however, no comparable downward adjustment in the remuneration of those executives who had appeared in the previous period to be overpaid. Ezzamel and Watson suggest that these results are consistent with the complaints of shareholder groups that remuneration committees have the effect of bidding-up executive pay, rather than strengthening the pay–performance link. They further suggest that a significant element of the bidding-up is probably related to the use of consultants by remuneration committees, who are likely to base their recommendations on comparisons with similar-sized firms. There may also, of course, be major demotivation problems if senior executives face pay reductions on the same basis.

These results are similar to those for the privatised water utilities (Ogden and Watson, 1996) where similar concerns about the pay–performance link have received extensive attention. Of concern for the process of setting remuneration, Ezzamel and Watson also show that the incidence of combined CEO–chairman posts remains extensive and that there is a high level of both membership and chairmanship of remuneration committees by executive directors. This evidence reflects that emerging from other studies (e.g. Conyon and Mallin, 1995). Notwithstanding the possibility that executive directors may 'leave the room' when their own remuneration is discussed, there clearly does remain concern about the process by which remuneration committees operate in pay determination.

While there would appear to be some cause for concern, it needs to be borne in mind that this study, as with much similar research in this area, focuses on a subset of the pay–performance relationship. Ezzamel and Watson measure remuneration in terms of salary plus bonus and exclude other important elements such as stock options and pension rights. Stock options in particular may constitute a variable element in remuneration that closely reflects company performance. It should not be forgotten that company performance is a reflection of the efforts of all the executive directors, not just the CEO. Hence, there would appear to be a strong need for further research in this area which captures these issues. Recent research which is now beginning to emerge (Main, Bruce and Buck, 1996) does show that when stock options are included, a much stronger pay–performance link can be identified. Research in this area would still appear to be hindered by the difficulties in obtaining full information on all aspects of executive remuneration, notwithstanding the Cadbury, Greenbury and other recommendations (e.g. Egginton, Forker and Grout, 1993) concerning disclosure, further efforts to enhance disclosure requirements would appear to be warranted. In early 1996 the government published a consultative document on proposed changes to the requirements of the Companies Act 1985 relating to the disclosure of directors' emoluments in order to remove overlap and ensure consistency with the Greenbury recommendations which may go some way towards addressing this issue, but clearly further research is required.

AUDIT COMMITTEES

Chapter 3 by Paul Collier examines the impact of audit committees in smaller listed companies. The cost of compliance with Cadbury may be raised in such companies as the burden may be substantially greater than for their larger counterparts. Issues are also raised which concern the potential for substitution of audit committees for other more effective monitoring systems, although, of course, their potential complementarity should not be forgotten. Colliers' findings highlight a number of short-comings in the workings of such committees in smaller listed companies. First, there was evidence that audit committees did not always strictly conform to the Cadbury model. Notably, there was a tendency for them not to have three non-executives primarily because of the smaller size of boards. Second, the excessive cost of appointing additional non-executives was often viewed as unjustifiable from a cost–benefit perspective. Third, the governance problems which emerged from the presence of executive directors on audit committees concerned the general absence of private meetings between auditors and only the non-executives. Collier also suggests that, on balance, the Cadbury audit committee recommendations appear to have reduced contact between the executive directors and the auditors.

Finance directors interviewed by Collier are generally in support of audit committees as they increased non-executives' involvement in critical business areas, they provided a forum for developing close relationships between non-executives and auditors and they enhanced the flow of information to directors. However, finance directors remained concerned that unscrupulous dominant personalities among executive directors could still choose non-executives who were not fully independent.

The positive views expressed by finance directors were also echoed by those of the non-executives, who saw membership of the audit committee as crucial in enabling them to ensure that the executives act in the interests of shareholders. They did not appear concerned that they may not have time alone with the auditor. They also took the view that the presence of the finance director was essential to the effective functioning of audit committees. Although they were generally satisfied with the time devoted to meetings, they did take the view that it was unrealistic to expect audit committees to fulfil all the functions recommended by Cadbury. The onus was seen to remain with the auditors to alert directors to major areas of concern.

In contrast to Colliers' findings in respect of smaller listed companies, in Chapter 4 Roger Mills shows that all the larger listed firms in his sample had an audit Committee made up entirely of non-executive directors. The duties of these committees were found to include recommending to the board the appointment of external auditors and their fees, reviewing financial statements prior to board review, setting the nature and scope of the audit with the external auditor and reviewing internal control systems. The process of the functioning of the audit committee in larger companies is less clear, however, and comparative evidence to that of Collier for their smaller counterparts would be useful.

INTERNAL CONTROLS

Although the Cadbury Committee recommended that companies should comment in their annual reports on the effectiveness of the companies' systems of internal control, the scope of this report has been the subject of some debate. Christine Mallin's survey of large companies in Chapter 5 finds evidence of concern over the difficulties in reporting on internal control. Finance directors of smaller listed companies interviewed by Collier also expressed concern that the additional costs imposed by the requirement to report on the effectiveness of internal controls would not be matched by the value added. Collier's non-executive sample took the view that Cadbury's recommendations on internal controls gave them responsibilities for areas outside their control.

A particular difficulty concerns the issue of what is to be included in the definition of internal control. The Cadbury Committee did not define internal control, but given its terms of reference appears to have had in mind an emphasis on internal financial controls. This was the view taken by the Working Group established to provide guidance to companies in this area and is in contrast to the US approach. The guidelines suggested that internal financial controls should embrace issues concerning the materiality and the likelihood of financial risks which may be incurred.

In large complex organisations, the problems of internal control are well recognised. There is an extensive literature which aims to identify the most appropriate control structures and processes for differing circumstances (see e.g. Otley, 1988, for reviews), with emphasis being given to the need to provide both financial and non-financial information in more uncertain, complex and dynamic environments. However, there may be serious difficulties in designing effective control systems which curtail opportunism by divisional management (Wright and Thompson, 1987). An interesting recent study of the control links between parents and subsidiaries by Jones, Rickwood and Greenfield (1993) echoes this view and shows the important need for parent–subsidiary control systems to provide parents with early warning signals of impending problems. They find, however, that second-tier managers regard the provision of such information, in addition to running the business, as creating a stressful and constantly changing burden which did not help them to run their divisions. They also show that subsidiary managers were typically encouraged to develop their own system which was more appropriate to their local needs and that informal information systems provided an important positive link between subsidiaries and the centre. The signals offered to parents provide an input into an overall assessment of the risks facing the business. However, these findings suggest that firms which use only a formalised and mechanistic approach to internal controls may well meet reporting requirements but it is doubtful whether effective corporate governance at the internal level will be achieved.

Mills' survey of finance directors of the largest 100 companies quoted on the London International Stock Exchange shows that in most cases internal control embraces both operational and financial controls. Moreover, finance directors reported that there was no clear distinction between operational and financial control.

Further problems are created by the need to report on the effectiveness of internal control mechanisms, which is itself influenced by the adopted definition of internal controls. Mills finds that while the largest single interpretation (31% of his sample) is consistent with the Working Party's Guidance for Directors, over a quarter of companies (27.7%) interpret effectiveness in terms of both financial and business controls. Mills also shows that companies see risk assessment, prioritisation and management as an essential aspect of internal control, but finds that the specifics of the process varied considerably between companies. His findings emphasise the importance of internal control systems which provide for risk assessment and management not only for accountability purposes but also as a basis for the identification of opportunities for the creation of value. There would appear to be scope for further analysis of the appropriate systems required to achieve such objectives.

INSTITUTIONAL INVESTORS

The Cadbury Report placed particular emphasis on the role of institutional investors in influencing standards of corporate governance. As the successor body to the Cadbury Committee, the Hampel Committee, came into operation, the role of institutional investors remained the subject of considerable debate. For example, the 100 Group, a committee of the finance directors of the largest UK companies, expressed particular concern about the ability of institutions to act properly as owners when they can sell their holdings in the short term (see the interview with the chairman of the 100 Group in Irvine (1996).

In their analysis of listed companies in the UK in Chapter 1 Short and Keasey show that the presence of institutional shareholders does have a positive effect on corporate performance by affecting the relationship between performance and other ownership interests. They do point out, however, that the relationship is a complex one. When considered independently of other ownership interests, they find no significant relationship between performance and institutional ownership. The presence of institutional shareholders may, however, curb management discretion by strengthening the positive relationship between performance and directors' ownership. In addition, there appears to be an interaction between institutional shareholders and other external shareholders. Institutional shareholders are found to have a significantly positive effect on performance only in the absence of other large external shareholders.

Cadbury recommended that institutional investors should disclose their policies on the use of voting rights. Mallin's interviews with institutional investors find that most have a policy of voting on all issues wherever possible, although a minority only vote on contentious issues. However, in a survey of the Top 250 companies Mallin finds that, on average, institutions' voting levels are only 35%. She also finds that there are important differences in the level of voting between different institutions. The twenty largest institutional investors in each company exhibit voting levels of 77.6% and 72.4% for insurance- and pension-related holdings, respectively. Mallin makes a number of recommendations for increasing the voting levels of institutional investors: requirements for companies to disclose the level of voting on each resolution at the last AGM; institutional investors to disclose their voting policy and the level of voting that they have achieved in the companies they invest in; *ex-post* analysis of their voting by institutions; industry-standard clauses in clients' contracts giving fund managers the discretion to vote the shares in accordance with their detailed voting policy statement; the dissemination to all investors of a guide to proxy voting; streamlining of the proxy voting procedures; companies to be informed of the person responsible for completing proxy forms; and companies to have a strong secretariat function to monitor and progress proxies.

Mallin's finding of differences in voting levels between different types of institution raises a potentially important issue. There has been a tendency to regard institutional investors as homogeneous, yet there are clear arguments to suggest that this is not so, with the result that differing impacts on corporate governance may be expected (see e.g. Charkham, 1994).

Hoskisson *et al.* (1995) distinguish between mutual funds and pension funds and argue that the former have shorter-term objectives than the latter who do not experience pressure for immediate returns. Moreover, they expect that differing objectives of different types of institutional investor will be systematically related to variations in strategy. They find that mutual funds prefer external acquisition of new products and processes as well as international diversification, since these are less risky and more short-term oriented than internal innovation. Pension fund managers, in contrast, are found to prefer internal innovation leading to new products in firms with focused strategies. It would be appropriate for further studies in the UK in order for comparisons to be made with this US evidence.

ENTERPRISE AND GOVERNANCE

Although the corporate governance debate has emphasised issues of accountability, the corporate governance framework and discussion out-lined earlier identified the importance of both enterprise and account-ability. Indeed, the results of the studies in this book draw attention to the difficulties in focusing on accountability in the absence of considerations of enterprise. The Director-General of the Institute of Directors has also emphasised the need for the successor body to the Cadbury Committee, the Hampel Committee, to have a wider remit which incorporates enterprise as a priority (Institute of Directors, 1996). The crucial question to be addressed concerns how the goals of accountability and enterprise might be achieved in the future.

It is clear from Figure I.1 that effective corporate governance involves a multi-faceted set of activities (e.g. Hart, 1995; Keasey and Wright, 1993) involving institutional investors, insider and outsider board membership and equity ownership, executives with appropriate performance-related remuneration, board committees, the market for corporate control, banks, etc. What is less clear is both the extent to which these activities may be both substitutes and complements, and whether governance affects strat-egy or whether firms match governance mechanisms to strategy.

Although there has been increasing debate about the substitutability of insider and outsider systems of corporate governance (for example, see Mayer, 1996) there are dangers in taking an oversimplified view which focuses on either one system or the other. Moreover, insider and outsider aspects each contain a heterogeneity of governance elements which may be in conflict. Mayer (1996) argues that it is likely that neither the insider nor the outsider system is universally better. They are each to be viewed as being suited to specific circumstances and industries, with insider systems better suited to cases where commitment to other stakeholders is important while outsider systems are more appropriate in cases where there is rapid change, technological progress and innovations in management systems. Essentially, part of the future debate on corporate governance will need to consider the relationships between strategy formulation, organisational structures and enterprise.

Illustrating the above arguments, research by Johnson, Hoskisson and Hitt (1993) suggests that there is substitution between governance mechanisms, notably ownership and board monitoring and internal managerial control. In their examination of large firms which have undergone voluntary restructuring, they found that outside board members only became involved in restructuring when managerial strategy implementation was deficient. They also showed that top management equity stakes and an emphasis on strategic (as opposed to financial) controls are negatively related to board involvement in restructuring. In respect of top management equity stakes, outside board members are less likely to be involved in restructuring as internal management are incentivised to take early action. On the other hand, an emphasis on strategic controls rather than financial controls allow managers to identify and correct problems on a real-time basis. Rediker and Seth (1995) question the evidence relating to the links between ownership concentration, board members' share-ownership and performance. They argue that performance depends on a bundle of governance mechanisms rather than on a single mechanism. Ownership concentration alone, for example, may not fully represent the efficiency of the bundle of governance mechanisms which are likely to be present in a particular business. Examining alternative internal governance mechanisms in bank holding companies they provide evidence of the substitutability of institutional investor ownership, mutual monitoring by inside directors, and incentive effects of shareholdings by managers.

In terms of corporate entrepreneurship, Baysinger and Hoskisson (1990) argue that outside directors (even those with equity ownership) may have a potentially negative impact on it. Outside directors may emphasise short-term performance through their reliance on financial rather than strategic evaluation of the business which results from their weaker access to detailed firm-specific information. They may also favour expansion through easier-to-evaluate external means rather than through internal mechanisms. Internal directors, in contrast, may be expected to have a stronger understanding of the business and may view internal development as less risky than do outside directors. Hence, governance involving a greater role for insiders may be more appropriate in situations of greater uncertainty, whereas outsiders may be more effective where the opposite is the case. In addition, there is little doubt that insider and outsider ownership are unlikely to be perfect substitutes across a range of situations. Although a start has been made on examining the links between structures and enterprise, it is clear that this will increasingly need the focus of future research and debate if the maximum benefits are to be reaped from changes in corporate governance mechanisms.

For example, even after making allowance for the above arguments, there remains the issue of whether insiders can be effectively monitored. If they cannot, then enhanced 'mechanisms of accountability' may achieve little and may be potentially damaging. Outsiders who become insiders may not necessarily be motivated to promote appropriate corporate governance and may be subject to the influence of dominant existing insiders. Franks and Mayer (1996) express concern that high levels of intercorporate holdings may create insider systems largely immune to sanction by outside investors. The increasing focus on insiders and active investors reflects considerable concern about the effectiveness of hostile takeovers as a disciplinary mechanism which ensures that managers perform. These views are often associated with arguments to restrict hostile takeovers. However, it is probably too simplistic to take either of the extreme views that hostile takeovers should be prohibited or should be regarded as the primary tool of corporate governance. For example, restrictions on takeovers may remove the potentially beneficial effects of a perceived takeover threat, whether or not that threat materialises (Chiplin and Wright, 1987; Markides, 1995; Wong, 1996). Franks and Mayer (1996) show that although hostile takeovers are less likely to be related to the correction of earlier poor performance, they are typically associated with considerable restructuring and managerial turnover as a form of *ex ante* correction. Moreover, though relatively few bids are overtly hostile, apparently agreed bids may mask initial approaches which are unwelcome to management who are underperforming and who may subsequently be removed.

There is recent evidence which suggests that the threat of takeover is associated with corporate restructuring attempts (Gibbs, 1993). However, to the extent that there are weaknesses in governance mechanisms, agency problems persist and it should not be surprising if managers continue to engage in acquisitions which are not value maximising. For example, evidence from major divestors in the UK shows extensive activity in the mid-1990s to unwind what were supposed to be value-enhancing acquisitions carried out in the late 1980s but which have turned out to be underperforming and ill-fitting (Wright and Robbie, 1996). It may be the case, for example, that enhancements to other elements of corporate governance, such as extensions to the requirements of bidder shareholders to vote on acquisitions above a certain size and to closer links between performance and executive remuneration, will provoke more value-enhancing acquisitions.

There have also been concerns about the role of banks in corporate governance, especially in an Anglo-American context. Bank debt can be seen as providing an important hard budget constraint and bankruptcy threat. It can be suggested that debtholders will only intervene when their investment is at risk and hence only poorly performing firms are subject to this control mechanism. However, in assessing the corporate governance roles of banks, a key issue is the relationship between banks and their customers. Some have argued (e.g. Charkham in IoD, 1996) that relationships have weakened significantly as corporate treasury departments have become profit centres. Whether this is good or bad for corporate governance is a mute point. For example, Mayer (1988) sees close relationships as comprising procedures for evaluating prospective borrowers, monitoring the performance of borrowers and reacting to instances of financial distress. Holland (1994) provides recent evidence of the development of close bank–customer relationships involving rich information flows, high loyalty and commitment between parties, expectations of fair dealing and longevity of relationships, and the use of extensive informal as well as formal contracts. In this situation, any weakening of the relationship would be potentially detrimental to effective governance.

An important subset of the bank–customer relationship concerns the operation of debt covenants. Rajan and Winston (1995) examine the role of covenants as a contractual device to increase lenders incentives to monitor. Covenants provide incentives for lenders to take action and obtain information on which to base action. A crucial issue in the operation of covenants is whether they involve a mechanistic reaction to a firm's financial distress or whether they form part of a close relationship. Evidence of the role of bank covenants in buy-out transactions shows the existence of important close relationships between banks and borrowers (Citron, Robbie and Wright, 1996), with the former intervening to various degrees according to the level of financial distress rather than the mechanistic reaction to the breach of covenants set on the basis of accounting ratios being maintained at certain levels.

In the light of suggestions that governance structures found in venture capital and management buy-out transactions should be used as a model for changing the UK system (e.g. Sykes, 1994) it is also instructive to examine evidence on the effectiveness of the various elements of their governance structures. MacMillan, Kulow and Khoylian (1989) show that differing levels of involvement in venture capital investments were not related to the nature of the operating business but to the choice exercised by the venture capital firm itself as to the general style it wished to adopt. There were, however, no significant differences in the performance of businesses subject to differing levels of involvement. Involvement levels may be related to skills levels, with there being indications that the general type of skills possessed by venture capital executives varies between types of venture capitalist, with those employed by captive funds tending to be more financial skills oriented while those employed by independents tend to have greater industrial skills (Beecroft, 1994). Evidence from the USA which specifically examined interactions between venture capitalists and CEOs finds that their intensity depends on the extent of venture capitalist–CEO goal congruence, the degree of the CEO's new venture experience, the venture's stage of development, and the degree of technical innovation it is pursuing (Sapienza and Gupta, 1994).

Increasingly, evidence from buy-out transactions points towards the important role of managerial equity stakes in driving performance improvements (Thompson and Wright, 1995). Leveraged recapitalisations, which simply substitute debt for equity in quoted companies, appear to raise shareholder value (Denis and Denis, 1992) but do not have as great an impact as LBOs which also encompass managerial equity ownership and active investor involvement (Denis, 1994). Thompson, Wright and Robbie (1992) find using UK data that the size of entrepreneurs' equity stakes is strongly significant, whereas investor control variables and leverage have relatively little influence. Phan and Hill (1995) show that management equity holdings as well as debt are positively associated with improved performance post-buy-out, but that the former has a greater impact than the latter for both periods of one and five years after buy-out. There is a positive association between managerial equity and performance over a five-year period after buy-out but not in respect of debt and performance. Wright, Thompson and Robbie (1992) for the UK and Zahra (1995) for the USA provide evidence of entrepreneurial actions following buy-out which emphasise the positive role of the incentive effect of equity ownership and not simply the reduction of agency costs.

CONCLUSIONS

There is no doubt that corporate governance has been one of the key business topics of the first half of the 1990s and it will continue to be so for the foreseeable future. Indeed, Sir Ron Hampel, chairman of the successor body to the Cadbury Committee, has called for a 'full and frank' debate on the structure and workings of UK corporations that delves into such difficult topics as board structure and shareholder responsibilities. As a means of informing this future debate, the studies presented in this book shed interesting and, in our view, important light on the impact of a number of important elements of the Cadbury recommendations and several aspects deserve particular emphasis.

First, while there may be widespread compliance with Cadbury, there is a danger that actions become simply box-ticking exercises and/or impose a cost burden on firms which outweighs any benefits. There is, therefore, a need for enhanced understanding of the processes by which enterprises are complying with Cadbury through detailed case study analysis. Pettigrew and McNulty (1995) have emphasised the importance of behavioural issues in understanding the effectiveness of non-executive directors in particular. The work by Collier in this book has provided especially useful insights with regard to audit committees. Similarly, the work of Short and Keasey, and Mallin in respect of institutional investors also provides steps in this direction.

Second, there is an important need to weigh accountability issues with the requirement to encourage managers to take entrepreneurial actions to create shareholder value. To some extent the narrow terms of reference of Cadbury may have led developments down the accountability path at the expense of the latter. These problems emerge from the studies reported here. Collier's study provides evidence of directors' concerns about the value-enhancing aspects of audit committees. Similarly, Mills' study relating to reporting on internal controls shows the emphasis by directors on both financial and non-financial issues. There is also evidence from Ezzamel and Watson that more needs to be done in terms of the link between the remuneration structures of executives and corporate performance.

Third, and following on from the second point, there is a greater need to understand the links between the different aspects of an overall corporate governance structure. Although recent progress has been made, there does not as yet appear to be sufficient clarity concerning both their substitutability and complementarity.

Fourth, although there is increasing emphasis on the role of non-executive or outside directors we still know little about their relative effectiveness in terms of the balance between accountability and the promotion of corporate entrepreneurship. Too much influence by outside directors with different access to information and different attitudes to risk from insiders may mean that strategies are pursued which do not fully realise the wealth-creation possibilities of corporations. Too little influence may mean that insiders are not adequately monitored.

It is hoped that the above issues will form part of the research and debate which should emanate from the Hampel committee. Some early impressions as to how far they will feature are as follows. With the aid of City backing, the unitary board structure of UK corporations has been largely outside the current debate. There are indications, however, that Hampel wants unitary boards to be compared to other alternatives (for example, the dual board structure of Germany). How far he is successful seems dependent upon whether the large companies (and the IoD) allow it to become a meaningful part of the debate.

Following Cadbury and Greenbury, non-executive directors now have a much greater role to play in corporate affairs. Their roles have been extended from one of advice to one where they are supposed to examine the actions of executives across a number of dimensions. Part of the future agenda should consider the compatibility of these joint roles within different structures and, moreover, how they impact upon corporate enterprise. To avoid the capture of non-executives by executives, it has been suggested that they be paid in shares and that a new form of non-executive director, with special regards to quasi-regulatory issues, be created. The roles of non-executives must form part of the wider governance debate that incorporates strategy, structure and enterprise.

One of the most active parts of the current debate has been the role of institutional shareholders. There have been calls for institutions to be forced to vote and to disclose their decisions. While such a response is understandable, Chapter 1 by Short and Keasey on institutional shareholdings and their paper on mandatory voting (1996b) throws some doubt as to how successful such moves would be. Nonetheless, given the size and importance of institutional shareholdings within UK corporate life, it is a topic which needs to be kept at the forefront of any future debates.

In terms of future debate, it is unclear what will be the focus on auditors. It seems likely, however, that the independence of auditors will be one topic that receives consideration. To date there has been some disquiet over the same firm of accountants acting as both auditors and consultants to a given business. Other potential issues concern how far auditors should be responsible for reporting on compliance to Cadbury and Greenbury, and whether the appointment of auditors should be the sole responsibility of non-executives. Not surprisingly, the large accountancy firms to do not seem overly keen on such changes being instigated.

Finally, the topic of corporate governance will only promote the wealth of the nation if there is constant reflection on the changes that have been made and the potential changes that can be made. The current text offers new research findings on a number of issues stressed by the Cadbury committee and they should form part of a wider review of governance practice and opinion within the UK. As stressed throughout this introduction, the debate will only move forward, however, if there is more emphasis given to the interrelationships between accountability, strategy, structure and enterprise; and, herein, lies the challenge.

REFERENCES

Baysinger, B. and Hoskisson, R. (1990) The composition of boards of directors and strategic control: effects on corporate strategy. *Academy of Management Review*, **15**, 72–87.

Beecroft, A. (1994) The role of the venture capital industry in the UK. In Dimsdale, N. and Prevezer, M. (eds), *Capital Markets and Corporate Governance*, Oxford: Oxford University Press.

Charkham, J. (1994) A larger role for institutional investors. In Dimsdale, N. and Prevezer, M. (eds), *Capital Markets and Corporate Governance*, Oxford: Oxford University Press.

Chiplin, B. and Wright, M. (1987) The logic of mergers: the competitive market in corporate control in theory and practice. IEA Hobart Paper 107.

Citron, D., Robbie, K. and Wright, M. (1996) Loan covenants and relationship banking: a study of MBOs in default. CMBOR Occasional Paper.

Conyon, M. and Mallin, C. (1995) A review of compliance with Cadbury. University of Warwick, mimeo.

Denis, D.J. (1994) Organizational form and the consequences of highly leveraged transactions: Kroger's recapitalization and Safeway's LBO. *Journal of Financial Economics*, **36**, 193–224.

Denis, D.J. and Denis, D. (1992) Managerial discretion, organizational structure and corporate performance. *Journal of Accounting and Economics*, **16**, 209–236.

Egginton, D., Forker, J. and Grout, P. (1993) Executive and employee share options: taxation, dilution and disclosure. *Accounting and Business Research*, **23**(91A), 363–372.

Franks, J. and Mayer, C. (1996) Hostile takeovers and the correction of managerial failure. *Journal of Financial Economics*, **40**(1), 163–181.

Gibbs, P. (1993) Determinants of corporate restructuring: the relative impact of corporate governance, takeover threat and free cash flow. *Strategic Management Journal*, **14**(S), 51–68.

Guth, W. and Ginsberg, A. (1990) Guest Editor's Introduction: Corporate Entrepreneurship. *Strategic Management Journal*, **11**(S), 5–16.

Hart, O. (1995) Corporate governance: some theory and implications. *Economic Journal*, May, **105**, 678–689.

Holland, J. (1994) Bank lending relationships and the complex nature of bank–corporate relations. *Journal of Business Finance and Accounting*, **21**(3), 367–393.

Hoskisson, R., Hitt, M., Johnson, R. and Grossman, W. (1995) The effects of internal governance and ownership control on corporate entrepreneurship. University of Texas A&M, mimeo.

Humphrey, C., Moizer, P. and Turley, S. (1993) The audit expectations gap in Britain: an empirical investigation. *Accounting and Business Research*, **23** No. 91A, 395–411.

Institute of Directors (1996) Enterprise and governance. Proceedings of a Conference held at the Institute of Directors, IoD, London.

Irvine, J. (1996) Given the power, hoping for glory: interview with Brian Birkenhead. *Accountancy*, March, 52–53.

Jensen, M.C. (1993) The modern industrial revolution, exit, and the failure of internal control systems. *Journal of Finance*, **XLVIII**(3), 831–880.

Johnson, R., Hoskisson, R. and Hitt, M. (1993) Board of directors' involvement in corporate restructuring. *Strategic Management Journal*, **14**(S), 33–50.

Jones, S., Rickwood, C. and Greenfield, S. (1993) Accounting control and management philosophies. Research Board, ICAEW, London.

Keasey, K. and Wright, M. (1993) Corporate governance: issues and concerns. *Accounting and Business Research*, **23**(91A), 301–313.

MacMillan, I., Kulow, D. and Khoylian, R. (1989) Venture capitalists involvement in their investments: extent and performance. *Journal of Business Venturing*, **4**, 27–47.

Main, B., Bruce, A. and Buck, T. (1996) Total board remuneration and corporate performance. *Economic Journal*, November, forthcoming.

Markides, C. (1995) Diversification, restructuring and economic performance. *Strategic Management Journal*, **16**(2), 101–118.

Mayer, C. (1988) New issues in corporate finance. *European Economic Review*, **32**, 1167–1189.

Mayer, C. (1996) There is a direct relationship between a country's system of corporate governance and its economic success. In Institute of Directors,

Enterprise and Governance: Proceedings of a Conference held at the Institute of Directors, IoD, London.

Ogden, S. and Watson, R. (1996) Changes in incentive structures and links with performance changes: some evidence from the privatised water industry in England and Wales. *Journal of Business Finance and Accounting*, July, **28**, 5 and 6, 721–751.

Otley, D. (1988) The contingency theory of management control. In Thompson, S. and Wright, M. (eds), *Internal Organisation, Efficiency and Control*, Deddington: Philip Allan.

Pettigrew, A. and McNulty, T. (1995) Power and influence in and around the boardroom. *Human Relations*, **48**(8), 845–873.

Phan, P. and Hill, C. (1995) Organisational restructuring and economic performance in leveraged buy-outs: an *ex post* study. *Academy of Management Journal*, **38**(3), 704–739.

Rediker, K. and Seth, A. (1995) Board of directors and substitution effects of alternative governance mechanisms. *Strategic Management Journal*, **16**, 85–99.

Robbie, K. and Wright, M. (1996) Management buy-ins: entrepreneurs, active investors and corporate restructuring. *Studies in Finance*, Manchester: Manchester University Press.

Sapienza, H. and Gupta, A. (1994) Impact of agency risks and task uncertainty on venture capitalist–CEO interaction. *Academy of Management Journal*, **37**, No. 6, 1618–1632.

Shleifer, A. and Vishny, R.W. (1991) Takeovers in the 60s and the 80s: evidence and implications. *Strategic Management Journal*, **12**(S), 51–59.

Short, H. and Keasey, K. (1996a) Management ownership and firm performance: evidence from the UK. University of Leeds, Working Paper.

Short, H. and Keasey, K. (1996b) Institutional voting in the UK. In Keasey, K. and Wright, M. (eds), *Corporate Governance: Responsibilities, Risks and Remuneration*. Chichester: John Wiley & Sons Ltd.

Sykes, A. (1994) Proposals for a reformed system of corporate governance to achieve internationally competitive long-term performance. In Dimsdale, N. and Prevezer, M. (eds), *Capital Markets and Corporate Governance*, Oxford: Oxford University Press, pp. 111–127.

Thompson, S., Wright, M. and Robbie, K. (1992) Management equity ownership, debt and performance: some evidence from UK management buy-outs. *Scottish Journal of Political Economy*, **39**(4), 413–430.

Thompson, S. and Wright, M. (1995) Corporate governance—the role of restructuring transactions. *Economic Journal*, **105**, May, 690–703.

Whittington, G. (1993) Corporate governance and the regulation of financial reporting. *Accounting and Business Research*, **23**, No. 91A, 311–320.

Wong, P. (1996) Governance by exit: an analysis of the market for corporate control. In Keasey, K., Wright, M. and Thompson, S. (eds), *Corporate Governance: Economic and Financial Issues*, Oxford: Oxford University Press.

Wright, M. and Thompson, S. (1987) Divestment and the control of divisionalised firms. *Accounting and Business Research*, Summer, **17**, No. 67, 259–267.

Wright M., Thompson S. and Robbie K. (1992) Venture capital and management-led leveraged buy-outs: a European perspective. *Journal of Business Venturing*, 7, 47–71.

Wright, M. and Robbie, K. (1996) Investor buy-outs: a new strategic option. *Long Range Planning*, October, forthcoming.

Zahra, S. (1995) Corporate entrepreneurship and financial performance: the case of management leveraged buy-outs. *Journal of Business Venturing*, **10**(3), 225–247.

1
Institutional Shareholders and Corporate Governance

HELEN SHORT and KEVIN KEASEY

INTRODUCTION

Within the general UK corporate governance debate, there is an increasing emphasis on the need for institutional shareholders to play an active role in the governance of companies. For example, the Cadbury Report (1992) notes that, 'Because of their collective stake, we look to the institutions in particular, with the backing of the Institutional Shareholders' Committee, to use their influence as owners to ensure that the companies in which they have invested comply with the Code' (para, 6.16). However, in many of the discussions of the need for an increased involvement by institutions in corporate governance issues, there has been a distinct lack of consideration given to the objectives of institutions and their willingness and ability to govern corporations actively. In particular, it is not clear that institutions, at least on an individual basis, have incentives to devote resources to active monitoring. Agency problems existing between the ultimate beneficiaries of institutional funds and the fund managers responsible for the investment of those funds may act to emphasise short-term profits at the expense of the longer-term corporate governance issues. Furthermore, it is unclear that the role of institutions as shareholders can be easily reconciled with their role as investors where

Corporate Governance: Responsibilities, Risks and Remuneration. Edited by Kevin Keasey and Mike Wright © 1997 John Wiley & Sons Ltd.

there is a duty to maximise the return for the beneficiaries of the funds that they invest.

The purpose of this chapter is twofold. First, it attempts to identify the objectives of institutions in respect of their ownership and investment behaviour, and considers whether institutions have either the ability and/ or incentives to become more actively involved in the governance of corporations. Second, the chapter considers the existing empirical evidence relating to the effect of institutional shareholders on corporate performance, and presents additional analysis, undertaken by the authors, of the effect of institutions on performance on a sample of UK companies.

The chapter is structured as follows. The next section briefly outlines the size and importance of institutional shareholdings in UK companies. The third section provides a general overview of the objectives of and the incentives facing institutions in respect of their twin roles as investors of funds and shareholders in UK companies. The willingness and ability of institutions to intervene actively in the governance of corporations is examined in the fourth section. In this section, particular reference is made to the effect of the size of institutional equity holdings on the incentives of institutions to intervene; the public good nature of active monitoring and the associated problem of free riding; and finally, the conflicts of interests faced by institutions when considering whether intervention is worth while. The fifth section considers the previous empirical evidence relating to the effect of institutional shareholders on corporate performance, and presents additional analysis, undertaken by the authors, of the effect of institutions on performance on a sample of UK companies. The final section presents conclusions.

INSTITUTIONAL SHAREHOLDINGS IN THE UK

Over the 1980s and 1990s individual equity ownership has continued to decrease in terms of the total percentage of equity owned from 54% in 1963 to less than 18% in 1993. The corollary to the declining proportion of total equity held by individual shareholders has been an increasing dominance of institutional shareholders. Financial institutions held approximately 62% of ordinary shares in 1993, this percentage having more than doubled since 1963 (CSO, 1994a). The major growth in institutional shareholders is mainly the result of the growth in pension funds and, less significantly, insurance funds. Life insurance and pension funds, valued at

£694.8 billion, accounted for approximately 49% of the financial assets of the personal sector at the end of 1992; whereas direct holdings of UK securities accounted for only 10.9% of personal financial assets (CSO, 1994b). One of the reasons the pension fund vehicle is favoured as opposed to personal portfolios of shares is the tax advantages presently accruing to pension contributions and pension benefits, as compared to personal equity holdings.

Given that the pension funds are the largest form of institutional investor (in terms of net asset value) and furthermore, that UK ordinary shares make up over half of their total portfolio of assets (CSO, 1994b), it is not surprising that UK equity holdings make up a significant proportion of the net assets of institutional investors. Clearly then, the performance of UK equities is a key determinant of the performance of the various institutions and this in itself might be behind the belief that the institutional investors should have, from a pure self-interest perspective, a role to play in the more effective governance of UK corporations. It is at this very juncture, however, that a key issue for consideration arises; namely, why has corporate governance become such a major issue at a time when institutional shareholdings have increased?

GENERAL OVERVIEW OF THE OBJECTIVES AND INCENTIVES OF INSTITUTIONS

The Cadbury Report places emphasis on the ability of market solutions rather than on external regulation to solve corporate governance problems, and relies on shareholders (institutional investors) to shake off their traditional apathy and take a more active interest in the companies they own. In order for institutions to adopt a proactive monitoring role, it is necessary that institutions view themselves as owners of UK corporations rather than viewing equity shares as short-term investment vehicles. Charkham (1990) argues that because many institutions view shares as 'commodities' with no intrinsic qualities other than that they can be readily tradable in an active market, the system of corporate governance as laid down in the Companies Act breaks down because directors cannot be accountable to shareholders who refuse to accept their role as shareholders.

Institutional investors are responsible to the owners of the funds which they invest. The institutional investing arrangements which exist in the UK mean that, with the exception of insurance companies investing their own insurance funds, funds are in general invested by fund managers rather than the beneficial owners of those funds. The trustees of pension funds have a fiduciary relationship with the beneficiaries of the pension fund, and must act in their best interests. In a similar vein, quoted insurance companies (such as the Prudential) have a responsibility to their own shareholders. In this context, institutional investors have a duty to maximise their investment returns. An important question to ask is whether the role of institutions as major shareholders in UK companies can be reconciled with their role as investors of funds, etc. In their role as major shareholders, the Cadbury Report expects institutions to take on the role of the large shareholder, who will monitor company management on behalf of smaller shareholders. Hence, in this context, institutions are expected to take a long-term view of their shareholding positions, and, where necessary, incur expense in intervening to correct mismanagement. However, in their role as investors, institutions need to be free to move funds around in order to find the best return for the beneficiaries of those funds. In this respect, it is difficult, certainly in the current ideological free-market climate, to argue that institutions should continue to hold equity positions in problem companies and incur additional expense intervening in management, particularly when there are no guarantees that intervention will be successful. Indeed Drucker (1976) argued that

'The pension funds are not 'owners', they are investors. They do not want control ... The pension funds are trustees. It is their job to invest the beneficiaries' money in the most profitable investment. They have no business trying to 'manage'. If they do not like a company or its manage-ment, their duty is to sell the stock' (p. 82).

From an alternative viewpoint, Hutton (1995) argues that 'Pension funds and insurance companies have become classic absentee landlords, exert-ing power without responsibility and making exacting demands upon companies without recognising their reciprocal obligation as owners' (p. 304).

As shareholders, it is, however, the right of institutions to appoint directors and, it could be argued, their 'moral duty' to ensure that companies are governed in the interests of shareholders. However, while Hutton suggests that institutions have obligations as owners, it is not clear, certainly under company law, what those obligations are, if indeed they do have obligations as owners. Furthermore, all shareholders are faced with a potential free-rider problem. If, for example, an institution took costly actions to intervene in company management while other institutions simply did nothing, the intervening institution would report lower returns (at least in the short term), to the detriment of its beneficiaries/ shareholders. If the intervening institution is a fund manager investing funds on behalf of external pension funds, given the increasing competition in fund management, the intervening manager is likely to lose clients. On the face of it, it is difficult to see what incentives there are for institutions to bear a private cost for a public good (for other shareholders, both private and institutional, and for the economy as a whole).

Cadbury (1990) argues, however, that while 'free riding' may be an option for individual institutional investors, for institutions collectively, this situation is becoming less tenable as the proportion of equity they own increases. The classic public good dilemma, therefore, arises in that because individual shareholders (institutions) do not have the appropriate mix of incentives to become involved in the detailed governance of corporations, the emphasis is on short-term gains at the expense of long-term corporate performance. The different types of institutions may, however, have varying time frames for their investment portfolios. For example, pension funds, who should have a long-term perspective because of the nature of their business, are more likely to emphasise the importance of achieving long-term corporate performance.

When examining the objectives of institutions and of their investment managers, the general investment environment in the UK needs to be considered. The nature of ownership in the UK is essentially short-term with equity shares seen as commodities (Charkham, 1990). Similarly, the relationship between the City and British industry has been essentially one of arm's length investment. The market for funds (both equity and debt) is seen essentially from a short-term perspective, with both sides of the funding transaction viewing the transaction in terms of price and availability. The arm's-length market nature of the system promotes an emphasis for both sides of the system that militates against active, direct governance from the providers of finance: the logic of the system is a market based upon exit rather than voice. However, it is within this system that the institutions are expected to have the motivation and ability to adopt active and direct governance.

Despite the fact that the nature of the market would seem to discourage monitoring, there are many examples of institutions having intervened in the management of problem companies (see Black and Coffee, 1994, for examples of institutional intervention and the circumstances surrounding such interventions). However, as Black and Coffee note, such intervention is usually carried out in private rather than in the public arena and, moreover, usually as a last resort in times of crisis. Hence, by its very covert nature, it is not presently possible to examine the degree to which institutions intervene in the governance of corporations nor the effect of any intervention.

.To summarise, it is clear that a problem exists in attempting to reconcile the role of institutions as shareholders with their role as investors of funds. Although in the long term and at a collective level, the objectives of institutions as both shareholders and investors should be to improve corporate performance (brought about, it is assumed, by improving the standards of corporate governance), in the short term and at an individual level, it is not clear that institutions' objectives from the investment perspective can be met by improving their role as shareholders.

THE WILLINGNESS AND ABILITY OF INSTITUTIONS TO INTERVENE IN THE GOVERNANCE OF CORPORATIONS

There is much anecdotal evidence to suggest that institutional share-holders do not adopt a monitoring role, preferring to sell their holdings in 'problem' companies rather than intervening in the management of that company (to 'exit' rather than use 'voice', in Hirschman's, 1970, terms). There are several reasons why institutions may adopt such a stance. First, if they intervene publicly, they are effectively drawing to public attention the difficulties the company is facing. This is likely to be perceived as 'bad news' by the market, resulting in a fall in share price and a reduction in the value of their investment. Second, if they become involved in the management of such 'problem companies', they become privy to inside information and unable to trade in those shares, potentially compounding their losses. Finally, effective monitoring is costly in terms of time and money, especially for institutional investors which hold diverse portfolios. To counter the above, it may be argued that the option of exiting becomes more problematic as institutional investors increase their stakes in public companies and as the number of institutional players in the market decreases. Selling large blocks of shares in an 'problem' company is likely to be extremely difficult, particularly as the potential buyer is likely to be an alternative institution with knowledge of the potential problems which exist in the company.

In this section the factors which affect the willingness and ability of the institutions to intervene to correct corporate governance failures (to use voice rather than exit) are evaluated. Specifically, this section considers the effect of the size of institutional equity holdings on the incentives of institutions to intervene; the public good nature of active monitoring and the associated problem of free riding; and finally, the conflicts of interests faced by institutions when considering whether intervention is worth while.

Effect of the Size of Institutional Holdings on Incentives

The Cadbury Report suggests that, by virtue of the size of their holdings, institutional investors have the potential to exercise considerable control over the actions of the board of directors—potential which is rarely available to other (small) shareholders. From a rational perspective, one aspect of the governance of corporations is that the costs of intervening must be less than the probable benefits of intervention if governance actions are to be effected. As Stiglitz (1985) argues, individual shareholders with relatively small holdings have little incentive to gather and bear the relatively fixed costs of collecting information to enable them to monitor and control the behaviour of the board. Alternatively, large shareholders may have sufficient incentives to obtain the information necessary to effectively control management if the benefits of such monitoring outweigh the associated costs. However, Stiglitz does note that control by large shareholders may have a cost; if such shareholders are limited in terms of their diversification, then their objectives may conflict with those of small shareholders. Furthermore, Stiglitz suggests that large controlling shareholders and managers may co-operate in the diversion of resources from remaining shareholders.

Notwithstanding the desirability of governance via large institutional shareholders and the fact that the benefit/cost ratio is likely to be more favourable for large as compared to small shareholders, there still remains the issue of whether the probable benefits of governance are likely to outweigh the mostly certain costs for large shareholders. Given the general direction of the relationships between firm size and benefits/costs, and the highly firm-specific nature of any individual relationship, this current issue reduces to a consideration as to whether given percentages of shareholdings enable institutions to alter the actions of corporations and thereby the probable benefits they receive. Although this is difficult to answer in the absolute, it is possible to form an impression from the current holdings of the UK institutions. While institutional investors as a collective own the majority of equity in UK companies, on an individual basis, their shareholdings are mostly in the region of 2–3% of issued shares. Clearly, institutional investors will be unwilling to take on substantially larger holdings of equity in a single company as that would effectively 'lock' them into that company, and potentially present liquidity and portfolio diversification problems.[1] While a shareholding in the region of 2–3% is large relative to individual shareholders, in comparison to the size of the company and that of institution's total portfolio, it is small and may not warrant the expense which has to be incurred in actively monitoring management. Nonetheless, the control potential of a shareholding by an individual institution needs to be taken in the context of City relationships and the potential to influence other institutions/shareholders. This will depend on the ability of an institution to marshal the support of other shareholders and this in turn is a complex function of the distribution of the size of other shareholders and their diversity of interests. Given the difficulties of determining the potential influence of a particular block of shares and in the absence of fully understanding the institutional dynamics of the City, it is a brave step to conclude that institutional investors have the potential to exercise considerable control over the actions of boards.

The argument so far has, however, ignored the actual size of the institutions and their general ability to influence general impressions within the share-buying market. There is no doubt that many of the financial institutions are large as measured by any yardstick. For example, the Prudential had a market value of £5436 million in June 1994, placing it in the top 30 companies quoted on the London Stock Exchange in terms of market value. Postel alone has £25 billion in funds under its control. This gives them a voice, via their impact upon the media, of considerable volume and a potential ability to influence general perceptions. Moreover, the potential for such public voice translates into private influence and the seeming willingness of corporations to manage specific sessions for institutional shareholders. The obvious benefits to be gained by corporations and institutional shareholders in ensuring 'control' is in the private rather than the public domain is one reason why it is difficult to gauge the influence of institutional shareholders. Thus, there is an argument which suggests that the large institutional shareholders may be able to influence the affairs of a corporation over and above their nominal shareholdings. This then moves us on to consider why the institutions bother monitoring the actions of individual companies when they can free ride on the actions of others.

The Free-rider Problem

The above sections have mentioned the free-rider problem facing individual institutions. This section considers, in more detail, the merit of applying free-rider type arguments to institutional investors. An absence of governance by institutions because of the potential for individual institutions to benefit from the actions of others is also indicative of a free-rider problem. Since the benefits of any collective action go to every individual in a group whether or not that individual has borne any of the costs of the collective action, it follows that, unless the group is small or meets certain other special conditions, the collective good will *not* be provided through market mechanisms or other straightforward and voluntary arrangements. Given that institutional investors are subject to such free-rider problems, it may be more relevant to examine why institutions ever engage in collective action when there are so many factors counting against such actions. For example, as Black and Coffee (1994) note, the absence of a generally accepted mechanism for cost sharing among institutions that undertake collective action presents a major obstacle to such collective action.

An analogy which may be applied to institutional investors to illustrate the nature of the conflict which might lie between private and collective benefits/costs is the famous Prisoners' Dilemma. The classic Prisoners' Dilemma relates the tale of two prisoners who have been caught in a joint crime. Each prisoner is interviewed separately by the judge and told 'I have enough evidence to send both of you to prison for a year if neither of you confess. However, if you alone confess, I'll send you to prison for just three months, while your partner will receive a ten-year sentence. If you both confess to the crime, you'll both be sentenced to five years in prison.' As neither prisoner knows what action the other prisoner will take, the likely outcome is that both prisoners will confess (avoiding the risk of a ten-year sentence), whereas the optimal solution (from the prisoners' collective point of view) would be for neither prisoner to confess.

However, there are major differences between the Prisoners' Dilemma and the framework within which institutions operate which may help to overcome the seemingly insurmountable free-rider problems facing institutional investors. However, before examining these differences in detail, it is necessary to note the environment in which the institutions operate. Another peculiar feature of the UK market for funds is its spatially concentrated nature within London's Square Mile. Historically, the investing institutions have a well-developed network of informal communication. Thus, one of the problems of trying to analyse and understand institutional governance in the UK is that it seemingly operates via a series of well-developed informal networks, usually behind closed doors. Thus although there may be a lack of publicly noted governance, this does not mean that governance actions do not occur. Therefore, when analysing the actions of institutions, it is necessary to take into account the nature of the relationships within the Square Mile. Moreover, from a corporate governance perspective, there are two ways of viewing the investing institutions' marketplace; as a no-holds barred competitive situation or as a competitive market underpinned by orderly conduct. All the available evidence (for example, see Holland, 1994) points to the latter being the most appropriate description. This suggests that, although the governance actions of institutions may be seen as being conditioned by a free-rider problem, the informal systems of the City allow collective solutions to be found. Thus, although the institutions may be seen as operating arm's-length investment policies, the history and nature of the City may allow governance issues to be confronted in 'relational' rather than pure arm's-length market terms.[2]

One feature of collective action to consider is whether the size of the group of institutional investors is an important factor in determining collective action. Specifically, would a sufficiently small group of institutional investors be able to overcome free-rider problems? The conclusion usually drawn from the Prisoners' Dilemma model is that even groups of only two members normally fail to obtain a collective good. It is only when two individuals repeat the Prisoners' Dilemma game a large number of times that they are able to achieve the gains from co-operation. In any single game (or in any set of games where the players know in advance how many games will be played), the dominant strategy for each player is to defect and not co-operate.

A crucial aspect of the Prisoners' Dilemma is that the prisoners are denied communication and hence the opportunity to make mutually advantageous deals. Clearly, such a situation does not exist within the City where there are well-developed networks (including the so-called 'old boys' network') and codes of practice and behaviour which have arisen from the City's long history of trading. Furthermore, within the context of the Prisoners' Dilemma, co-operation derives from the repeated play of a two-person game. Given that relationships which exist between the various institutions are generally long-term ones, there are incentives for institutions to take a long-term view of co-operation in corporate governance matters. For example, institutions may take turns to play the role of 'lead institution' when intervention in a company becomes necessary (see Black and Coffee, 1994, for a summary of the process of forming coalitions of institutions to confront management). If individual institutions refuse to play their part, it would seem likely that other institutions will withdraw their goodwill towards that institution and refuse to co-operate in future interventions. Hence, the existence of communication networks and the long-term nature of mutually advantageous relationships between City institutions may contribute towards an environment in which co-operation can take place and free riding is reduced.

However, within the context of the Prisoners' Dilemma, the tendency towards co-operation is diminished as group size increases. In a sufficiently large group where no single member gets no more than a small share of the benefits of a collective good, the incentive to co-operate with other potential beneficiaries of the collective good disappears. In support of this, Black and Coffee (1994) note that when institutional coalitions do form, they are usually small in terms of the number of institutional participants but relatively large in terms of collective shareholding. However, although the communication and interaction networks within the City works may appear to reduce free riding, the increasing number of institutions within the City may help to break down the old codes of conduct and means of doing business (the evolving detail of the Barings crisis lends considerable weight to this perspective).

Although coalitions between institutions do form, those coalitions still face free-rider problems from institutions who do not form part of the coalition. In the majority of situations, it is likely that institutions involved in collective action against an individual firm will not be rewarded by substantial future profits from that firm. Furthermore, when the costs of taking such public action and the possibility that any action will be unsuccessful are taken into consideration, there remains the question of why institutions undertake such action when the benefits of doing so appear to be so small, if indeed any benefits exist. Public action is likely to be more costly than private action, as the very fact that public action has been taken suggests that previous 'behind the scenes' attempts to influence boards have failed. In addition, the particular institutions involved in such public action risk a loss of reputation if they are unable to force their desired outcomes. Given that public action is taken, albeit rarely, this suggests that there are some benefits to be gained, although these benefits may not be directly associated with the immediate action being taken against an individual firm. Rather, it is likely that action is taken to act as a deterrent to other companies' boards and to signal to the corporate community in general that intervention by institutions remains a credible threat.

Therefore, although it may be first assumed that institutions have very little incentive to become involved in the monitoring activities that corporate governance demands, it would appear that the relationships which exist between institutions act to limit free-riding behaviour. If collective action by institutions were to be viewed as a single play of the Prisoners' Dilemma game, it is clear that such collective action would be unlikely to take place due to the prevalence of free riding. However, given the City context in which the institutions operate, repeated play of the Prisoners' Dilemma is the more appropriate analogy to make, where co-operation between institutions becomes worth while. Furthermore, in the context of private versus public action, it would seem that, in the majority of cases, private action on the part of institutions would be the most appropriate course for institutions to take. However, when public action does occur, it is likely to be motivated by the need to enforce the notion that institutional intervention remains a credible threat.

Therefore, in summary, the public good nature of corporate governance actions and the associated incentives for free riding would suggest that monitoring would not be provided. However, the rationality arguments do not take into account the institutional framework of the Square Mile that has evolved over a number of centuries. The institutional investors in the UK form a highly concentrated network, often operating in the confines of the Square Mile with a well-developed history of relationships and communication. This facilitates the operation of relational dynamics and the possibility of concerted/focused action. In this form of society, it may, of course, be extremely difficult to directly identify actions that could be definitely categorised under the banner of governance; actions taking place through gentle persuasion and the knowledge that the potential public disclosure of opinions can be extremely damaging. In fact, the tendency to work behind closed doors in the UK reinforces the strength of any potential threat to 'go public'. Such a threat, of course, is only likely to be credible if the companies believe it is in the interests of the institutions to publicly voice their concerns. It is clear, however, that the nature of governance within the UK is such that it is difficult to visibly determine how far it is in operation. In addition, the problems of co-ordinating collective action mean that such actions occur only in extreme circumstances.

Conflicts of Interest

While there may be informal mechanisms in place which mean that institutions do have incentives to take governance actions (albeit in private rather than public), there are additional factors which provide disincentives to institutional monitoring and intervention. This section examines the possible conflicts of interests that certain institutions may face as a result of other (actual or potential) relationships with the company.

Pound (1988) presents three different hypotheses which may explain the relationship between institutions and their incentives to intervene in corporate governance—the efficient monitoring hypothesis, the conflict of interest hypothesis and the strategic alignment hypothesis. The efficient monitoring hypothesis suggests that institutional shareholders are more informed and able to monitor management at lower cost than small shareholders. Alternatively, the strategic alignment hypothesis suggests that institutional shareholders and the board may find it mutually advantageous to co-operate on certain issues. In a similar vein, the conflict of interest hypothesis suggests that institutional shareholders may have current or potential business relationships with the firm which make them less willing to curb management discretion actively.

Pound's hypotheses that the extent of institutional intervention will depend on the relationship between the institution and the company may be used to explain Postel's campaign against directors' three-year rolling contracts, a campaign which was unusual in that attempts to impose governance standards on companies were carried out in public, rather than using the generally preferred 'behind-the-scenes' method. Postel represents only two pension funds, the Post Office and British Telecom, and acts as their in-house fund manager. They are not open to business from any other sources and therefore do not have conflicts of interest which may preclude them from actively opposing management. Other pension fund managers such as merchant banks and insurance companies may have other business interests with the companies in question and hence are less likely to oppose management actively for fear of jeopardising those interests. In addition, fund management is a highly competitive business, and fund managers may understandably feel wary of criticising the very directors of a company whose pension fund management business they may be seeking in the future. It is notable that at the start of their campaign, Postel could not get open support from the umbrella organisations, the Association of British Insurers and the National

Association of Pension Funds, although this has changed, particularly since the publication of the Greenbury Report. Furthermore, many of the institutional investors are themselves quoted companies and have directors on three-year rolling contracts (a good example at the time was the Prudential). Hence, it could be argued, in line with Pound, that not only do such institutions face conflicts of interest but also that directors of institutions have reasons for aligning themselves with company management over certain issues for fear of specific practices, which they themselves adopt, becoming unacceptable. In addition, institutions may face conflicts of interest by virtue of their own ownership structure. In particular, certain fund-managing institutions are subsidiaries of investment banks. In such situations, conflicts of interest may arise between the institution and its parent with regard to corporate governance matters. Actions to curb management discretion by the institution may have long-term consequences for its parent if it has current business relationships with the firm or is likely to act as an advisor to the firm on future matters such as takeovers, rights issues, etc.

However, although there are obvious disincentives as a result of conflicts of interest to institutions becoming involved in governance issues, there are examples of direct involvement which suggest that the disincentives are not insurmountable and institutions do find it worth while to voice their concerns. For example, Postel is a particularly useful example of an institution that finds the benefits of open intervention to outweigh the costs. As Britain's largest in-house pension fund investor, it is estimated to own $1\frac{1}{2}\%$ of British industry and owns shares in a large percentage of all quoted companies. Therefore, the cost to firms of large compensation payments in the event of a director's loss of office as a result of three-year rolling contracts directly affects the fund's revenues. Its campaign focuses on one issue which is common to all companies, and hence the costs of intervention are much less than if it campaigned on individual firm-specific issues.

Pension funds such as Postel have characteristics which are similar to Coffee's (1991) notion of the 'optimal corporate monitor'. Coffee suggests that the optimal corporate monitor should be relatively free from conflicts of interest such that its monitoring and control activities are not biased by opportunities to earn other income from the company in question. It should also have a long-term investment horizon and its stake in the corporation should be large enough to justify the expenditure of significant monitoring costs. Coffee argues that pension funds are in a better position than other institutions to perform this role. However, while this is true of in-house managed pension funds such as Postel, the position is not so clear in the case of externally managed pension funds.

Furthermore, large pension funds tend to be highly diversified with relatively small holdings in any one company which places constraints on the amount of monitoring activity which can be undertaken, in terms of both cost and in-depth knowledge of management. In addition, the trustees of pension funds managed internally may face pressure from their own company's management to form strategic alliances with the management of the companies in which they invest. Their own companies may be faced with corporate governance problems to which they would rather not draw attention. Thus the point to note is that the institutions themselves are organisations where there is a separation between management and owners and hence the same potential governance problems are as likely to apply here as they are to corporations. Essentially, in promoting institutions as a partial solution to the governance problem, there is an inherent belief that institutions themselves are less prone to governance issues than corporations.

While there has been much debate concerning the ability of institutions to monitor corporate management effectively, relatively little attention has been paid to the monitoring of institutions themselves. As Jenkinson and Mayer (1992) argue: 'Why precisely managers of institutional funds are supposed to be so much better at administrating non-financial enterprises than the management of these enterprises themselves, or why similar problems of corporate governance do not afflict the funds themselves are questions that are never very clearly answered' (p. 2). Indeed, Coffee (1991) suggests that there are reasons to believe that some institutional investors are less accountable to their owners than are corporate managers to their shareholders, and argues that the usual mechanisms of corporate accountability are limited or unavailable at the institutional level. The extent of the problem depends on the nature of the institution concerned. For example, self-administered occupational pension schemes are obviously immune from mechanisms such as takeovers. In addition, their beneficiaries, the company's employees, are not in the position to sell their stakes in the pension fund if the fund underperforms. Furthermore, discipline in the form of monitoring by debtholders does not affect self-administered occupational pension funds.

In summary, institutions face conflicts of interest in their dealings with companies as a result of their role as shareholder/investor and current or potential business service provider, which possibly inhibits their willingness to apply pressure to company management in the event of corporate governance deficiencies. Furthermore, it is clear that the institutions themselves are not immune from corporate governance problems and may be unwilling to draw attention to these problems by criticising the companies in which they invest.

GOVERNANCE BY INSTITUTIONAL SHAREHOLDERS: EMPIRICAL EVIDENCE

We concentrate here on the empirical evidence relating firm performance to institutional shareholdings. In this regard, we first consider the prior evidence and then we present the results of our own recent empirical work on the subject.

Firm Performance and Institutional Shareholdings: Prior Empirical Evidence

Empirical investigation of the relationship between ownership/control structure, in terms of the identity of shareholders, and firm performance essentially attempt to test the managerial/agency theory propositions that different ownership/control structures result in differing performance (see Short, 1994, for a review of the relevant literature). Furthermore, it is assumed that if certain shareholders are acting as monitors of management behaviour (either actively or by virtue of their mere presence), performance will be better than in firms where monitoring does not occur (assuming that managers will not operate efficiently if monitoring does not take place). Much of the empirical literature utilises ownership stakes of institutional shareholders as a proxy for their willingness and ability to undertake monitoring activities. Ideally, the level of institutional activity with respect to intervention in board decision making, etc. and its subsequent effect on corporate performance should be examined, but such information is rarely publicly available. However, when examining the empirical evidence on the effect of institutions on corporate performance, it is essential that the limitations associated with such research are borne in mind when attempting to draw conclusions from such work.

There are a number of empirical papers which examine the relationship between firm performance and large shareholders in general (of which institutional investors may be seen as one identifiable group). With respect to the effect of large external shareholders, in general, on firm performance, the evidence is inconclusive. Holderness and Sheehan (1988), Murali and Welch (1989) and Denis and Denis (1994) found no evidence to suggest that performance differed between majority-owned firms and diffusely owned ones. McConnell and Servaes (1990) found blockholder ownership to have an insignificant effect on performance when considered independently of other ownership interests. However, when blockholder ownership and director ownership were combined, a significant relationship was reported. Overall, their results do not support the notion that large block ownership plays an important role in monitoring management. However, Zeckhauser and Pound (1990) reported results which suggested that the technical nature of the industry in which the firm operates had an effect on the ability of large shareholders to provide effective monitoring.

Little empirical evidence exists which examines the role of institutional shareholders in monitoring the board of directors and that which does exist has produced conflicting results. Investigating proxy contests, Pound (1988) reported results which indicated that institutions did not act as efficient monitors, providing evidence to suggest that institutions were more likely to vote in favour of management. This suggests that institutions either face conflicts of interest or find it worth while to align themselves strategically with the current management. Alternatively, Brickley, Lense and Smith (1988) examined institutional voting patterns in management-initiated anti-takeover amendments and found institutional opposition to be greatest when the proposal reduced shareholder wealth. In addition, their results suggested that institutions that are less subject to management influence, such as mutual funds and public pension funds, are more likely to oppose management than institutions, such as banks and insurance companies, who may have current or potential links with the firm. Therefore, although these findings are consistent with the efficient monitoring hypothesis, they do suggest that the conflict of interest hypothesis may hold for certain institutional shareholders. McConnell and Servaes (1990) found the percentage of shares owned by institutions to be positively and significantly related to Tobin's Q and that institutional ownership acted to reinforce the positive effect of directors' shareholdings on firm performance, a result they suggested was consistent with the efficient monitoring hypothesis. However, Chaganti and Damanpour (1991) found institutional ownership to have a significantly positive effect on the return on equity but not on other measures of firm performance (return on assets, price earnings ratio and total stock return).

Institutional Shareholdings and Firm Performance: New Empirical Results

This section presents new empirical results concerning the relationship between corporate performance and institutional shareholdings. In presenting the results, the section has the following structure. Subsection (a) describes the data and sample to be analysed, and (b) presents the dependent and explanatory variables. The univariate and multivariate results are presented in subsections (c) and (d), respectively.

(a) Data and Sample Selection

The hypotheses to be tested examine the effect of institutional shareholdings on corporate performance. In general, the empirical approach taken here is to investigate whether corporate performance is affected by the *presence* of institutional investors; that is, the percentage of shareholdings held by institutions and the changes over time in institutional shareholdings. Given such an approach, the basic hypothesis examined here is that corporate performance is a function of the firm's ownership structure and other control variables. However, before going on to discuss the hypotheses in depth, it is necessary to outline the form of the data which is available regarding the level of institutional shareholdings in a firm. Data on institutional ownership were extracted from the firm's annual reports. The available data on ownership contained in the annual report is determined by the Companies Act 1985, Part VI. Briefly, prior to 1990 the legislation required that details of external interests (that is, excluding directors' interests) which amounted to 5% or more (3% or more post June 1990) of the issued share capital to be disclosed. The cut-off point of 5% for disclosure is problematic as it naturally excludes ownership interests of less than this figure. As a consequence, any measure of the combined holding of institutions in a particular firm can only measure the combined holdings of institutions owning shares of 5% or more. This does provide a reasonable measure of shareholder concentration and potential control if it is assumed that only the larger institutional shareholdings will have incentives to act in unison to curb management discretion. However, it is quite possible that a firm which has no institutional shareholders individually owning above 5% has a total institutional shareholding above that figure. In such cases, given the data availability, these firms would effectively show an institutional shareholding of zero. However, it should be noted that the majority of previous empirical studies in both the UK and the USA suffer from similar problems.

In examining the relationship between performance and institutional shareholdings, there is a need to control for the potential effects of other shareholdings on firm performance. In particular, variables must be included which control for directors' shareholdings and other external shareholdings (see Short, 1994, for a discussion of the theoretical and empirical evidence regarding the effect of directors' ownership and other external ownership on firm performance, and papers by Morck, Shleifer and Vishney (1988), McConnell and Servaes (1990) and Leech and Leahy (1991)). Furthermore, in the light of Zeckhauser and Pound's (1990) contention that the degree of asset specificity (specifically, R&D expenditure) affects the ability of external shareholders to monitor firms, variables will be included to control for R&D expenditure. Variables are also included to control for other monitoring instruments, in particular, non-executive directors (Fama, 1980; Weisbach, 1988) and debt (Grossman and Hart, 1982; Jensen, 1986).

The sample was chosen from all UK firms quoted on the Official List of the London Stock Exchange for the period 1988 to 1992. In order to be included in the sample, the firms had to be quoted on the Official List for at least a year before the date of their accounting year end for 1988. This condition was imposed in order to ensure that performance and capital structure were not affected as a result of a new listing. In addition, ownership structure is likely to change as a consequence of a new listing. The basis of selection was random, subject to the following exclusions:

1. Firms in the financial and oil and gas sectors were excluded due to the different income-measuring rules governing such companies, as compared to those in the manufacturing and service sectors.
2. Privatised firms (such as water, electricity, etc.) were excluded as their operating conditions (in terms of regulation and monopoly markets) are usually atypical.
3. Firms in the broadcasting sector were excluded due to regulatory nature of the sector and the changes in regulation which occurred during the period.
4. Firms with ownership structures which did not conform to the typical one vote for each ordinary share were also excluded.

Having excluded firms on the above basis, a final sample of 225 firms was derived.

(b) Variables

The main variables used in the analysis are described below and presented
in Table 1.1. All variables, with the exception of ownership variables are
measured as averages over the period 1989 to 1992 and are inflation
adjusted via the RPI in 1990 pounds sterling.

Table 1.1   Firm Performance—Description of Variables

Variables	Description
Dependent variables	
VAL	Market value at the accounting year end, divided by the book value of equity at the accounting year end.
SHRET	$\ln\left[(P_t + d_t)/P_{t-1})\right]$ where P = share price and d = dividend per share.
CHANGEMV	$\ln(MV_t/MV_{t-1})$ where MV = market value.
RSE	Return on shareholders' equity equal to profits attributable to shareholders divided by shareholders' equity and reserves.
RSEREM	Return on shareholders' equity before the deduction of directors' remuneration, equal to profits attributable to shareholders + directors' remuneration, divided by shareholders' equity and reserves.
OPROFTA	Operating profit divided by total assets.
Ownership variables	
INSTPER	Percentage of shares owned by institutions owning 5% or more.
INSTDUM	Dummy coded 1 if institutional shareholders owning 5% or more is present, 0 otherwise.
DIR	Percentage of shares held beneficially and non-beneficially by directors.
RELATED	Percentage of shares held by ownership interests connected to directors.
EXTERNAL	Percentage of shares held by other external ownership interests.
BOARD	Number of executive directors divided by total board size.
Control variables	
SIZE	Log of firm sales.
BETA	Beta.
GROWTH	Growth in sales.
DEBT	Total debt divided by book value of equity.
RDSALES	Research and development expenditure divided by sales.
FASALES	Fixed assets divided by sales.
DIVERS	Sum of squares of proportions of sales in different (SIC three-digit) product classifications.
INDDUM1– INDDUM8	Industry dummies.

Dependent Variables—Performance

The following analyses use both measures of market and accounting performance. The market measures used are a valuation ratio (*VAL*), shareholders' return (*SHRET*) and the change in market value (*CHANGEMV*). The valuation ratio *VAL* is that used by Leech and Leahy (1991) and is calculated as the market value of the firm at its accounting year end, divided by the book value of equity at the accounting year end. Due to the skewness in the distribution of *VAL*, the log form of the variable is used throughout the analysis. *VAL* provides a measure of management's ability to generate a certain income stream from an asset base. If ownership structure, however, has an influence on both accounting performance (through reserves) and market value, then there will be cancelling effect, no matter how small, on both the numerator and denominator of the *VAL* variable. Hence additional market variables, outlined below, which are not subject to accounting methodology are also considered in the analysis.

Shareholders' return (*SHRET*) is calculated as $\ln[(P_t + d_t)/P_{t-1}]$ where P_t is the share price at the end of the period, P_{t-1} is the share price at the beginning of the period and d_t is the total dividend declared during the period. The change in market value (*CHANGEMV*) is calculated as $\ln(MV_t/MV_{t-1})$ where MV_t is the market value at the end of the period and MV_{t-1} is the market value at the beginning.

The accounting-based measures of performance are the return on shareholders' equity calculated both before and after the deduction of directors' remuneration (*RSEREM* and *RSE*). The return on shareholders equity is calculated both before and after the deduction of directors' remuneration because it is possible that ownership may have different effects on performance and remuneration. The exclusion of remuneration allows the testing of the effect of ownership on performance without any possible contamination of the relationship caused by the effects of ownership on remuneration. The final accounting measure is the ratio of operating profit to total assets (*OPROFTA*).

Explanatory Variables

Ownership Variables

In the analysis that follows, all ownership variables are defined as at the beginning of the period under analysis, that is, at the beginning of the firm's 1989 accounting year (and hence taken from the 1988 year-end annual report).

Directors' Ownership (DIR)   Directors' ownership (*DIR*) is measured as the percentage of equity shares beneficially and non-beneficially owned by directors and their immediate families at the beginning of 1989. Jensen and Meckling (1976) argue that directors' ownership helps to align the interests of directors with those of external shareholders, hence reducing the incentives of directors to consume excessive perquisites. On this basis, a positive relationship is expected to exist between firm performance and directors' ownership. However, Morck, Shleifer and Vishney (1988) and McConnell and Servaes (1990, 1995) find evidence of a non-linear relationship between performance and directors' ownership. In view of these findings, the relationship between firm performance and directors' ownership is *a priori* unsigned.

Institutional ownership (INSTPER)   Institutional ownership (*INSTPER*) is measured as the percentage of shares owned by institutional share-holders holding 5% or more of shares at the beginning of 1989. In addition, a dummy variable *INSTDUM* is coded 1 if any institutional shareholders own 5% or more of shares and 0 otherwise. As noted previously, Pound's (1988) 'efficient monitoring' hypothesis predicts that institutional shareholdings will have a positive effect on firm perform-ance. Alternatively, Pound's 'conflict of interest' and 'strategic alignment' hypotheses suggest that a negative relationship may exist between firm performance and institutional shareholdings.

Ownership interests related to directors (RELATED)   Related interests (*RELATED*) is measured as the percentage of shares owned by persons related in some way to the directors. Related interests include directors' family trusts (not included in directors' beneficial or non-beneficial holdings), members of directors' non-immediate family and ex-directors (unless it was clear that such directors resigned as a result of conflict with the remainder of the board). The relationship between firm performance and *RELATED* is *a priori* unsigned, as it is not clear whether related ownership interests will act to deter management inefficiency (and hence have a positive effect on performance) or will align themselves with management (and hence have a negative effect on performance).

Other external ownership (EXTERNAL)   Other external ownership (*EXTERNAL*) is measured as the percentage of shares owned by other external shareholders not included in other categories. This is a residual category and includes ownership by corporations, charities and individuals. As so-called large external shareholders with incentives to monitor management, a positive relationship is expected to exist between firm performance and *EXTERNAL*, although the results of empirical studies by Holderness and Sheehan (1988), Denis and Denis (1994) and McConnell and Servaes (1990) throw doubt on the ability of large external blockholders to monitor management.

Board structure (BOARD)   The variable *BOARD* is defined as the number of executive directors as a percentage of the total number of directors on the board. The Cadbury Report argued that non-executive directors are an essential component of the drive to improve corporate governance. However, the empirical evidence on the effect of board structure on various aspects of firm performance has produced mixed results. For example, Weisbach (1988), Hermalin and Weisbach (1988) and Rosenstein and Wyatt (1990) reported evidence to suggest that non-executive directors do provide an effective monitoring role. Furthermore, Pearce and Zahra (1992) found a positive relationship between the percentage of non-executive directors on the board and firm performance although Hermalin and Weisbach (1991) found no significant relationship.

Control variables   The variables utilised as control variables in the following analysis are described in Table 1.1. Briefly, these variables are firm size, risk, growth, product diversification, capital intensity of technology, debt, research and development expenditure and industry classification. These control variables were chosen due to their use in previous research of this type (in particular, see Leech and Leahy, 1991).

(c)   Univariate Statistics

Table 1.2 presents summary statistics relating to the distribution of ownership across the sample. It is clear from the table that institutional ownership concentration has increased dramatically across the period. Mean ownership increased from 7.73% in 1988 to 15.67% in 1992, and the median from 5.47% in 1988 to 14.50% in 1992. In addition, the average size of the largest institutional shareholder increased from 5.12% to 8.01% over the period. The percentage of firms in which a large institution is present increased from 57.3% in 1988 to 83.1% in 1992. Overall, these figures suggest that, in general, institutional shareholder concentration has increased over the period.

  In terms of directors' ownership, it would appear that the percentage of equity owned by directors has decreased slightly over the period. In 1988, the mean ownership was 13.34% which compares to a mean of 11.47% in 1992. General comparisons between directors' and institutional shareholdings indicate that in 1988, directors, on average, represented the largest block of shareholdings whereas, by 1992, large institutional share-

Table 1.2(a) Ownership Variables—Summary Statistics

	1988	1989	1990	1991	1992
Directors' beneficial and non-beneficial					
Mean	13.344	13.449	12.905	11.731	11.473
Median	5.260	6.745	6.270	5.590	4.110
Standard deviation	16.279	16.093	15.394	14.657	15.495
Minimum	0.000	0.000	0.000	0.000	0.000
Maximum	62.860	62.030	57.540	57.580	75.250
Related to directors'					
Mean	2.022	1.980	2.106	2.404	2.485
Median	0.000	0.000	0.000	0.000	0.000
Standard deviation	6.078	5.931	5.579	6.382	6.986
Minimum	0.000	0.000	0.000	0.000	0.000
Maximum	40.060	40.060	41.240	40.740	41.270
Institutional shareholders owning 5% or more					
Mean	7.728	9.382	12.427	14.418	15.674
Median	5.470	6.075	9.070	12.630	14.500
Standard deviation	9.380	10.421	11.635	12.480	12.618
Minimum	0.000	0.000	0.000	0.000	0.000
Maximum	45.470	47.250	50.100	59.900	62.800
Size of largest institutional shareholder owning 5% or more					
Mean	5.122	5.608	6.636	7.395	8.008
Median	5.430	5.900	6.740	7.180	7.300
Standard deviation	5.446	5.421	5.122	5.357	5.213
Minimum	0.000	0.000	0.000	0.000	0.000
Maximum	26.200	24.890	24.890	24.890	24.890
Size of five largest institutions owning 5% or more					
Mean	7.673	9.302	12.318	14.272	15.461
Median	5.470	6.075	9.070	12.630	14.130
Standard deviation	9.256	10.230	11.404	12.239	12.286
Minimum	0.000	0.000	0.000	0.000	0.000
Maximum	39.260	42.700	45.100	52.700	55.000
Other external shareholders					
Mean	6.869	6.838	7.326	7.487	6.650
Median	0.000	0.000	0.000	0.000	0.000
Standard deviation	14.938	14.519	15.135	16.134	15.779
Minimum	0.000	0.000	0.000	0.000	0.000
Maximum	93.900	79.800	80.030	85.330	85.330

Table 1.2(b) Presence of a Shareholder Owning 5% or More

	1988		1989		1990		1991		1992	
	No.	%	No.	%	No.	%	No.	%	No.	%
Institutional shareholders	129	57.3	138	61.3	164	72.9	173	76.9	187	83.1
Other external shareholders	72	32.0	69	30.7	74	32.9	73	32.4	63	28.0

holders represented the largest block. The figures for institutional share-holders clearly shows that institutions represent the most important external ownership interests, both in terms of presence and concentration.

Statistics relating to the structure of the boards of the sample companies are presented in Table 1.3. In terms of total size, boards have remained remarkably stable over the five-year period, averaging approximately

Table 1.3 Board Structure: Summary Statistics

	1988	1989	1990	1991	1992
Board size					
Mean	7.404	7.558	7.573	7.453	7.364
Median	7.000	7.000	7.000	7.000	7.000
Standard deviation	2.560	2.548	2.496	2.431	2.299
Minimum	3.000	3.000	3.000	3.000	3.000
Maximum	18.000	18.000	17.000	16.000	17.000
Number of executive directors					
Mean	5.004	5.054	4.969	4.747	4.618
Median	5.000	5.000	5.000	5.000	4.000
Standard deviation	2.010	1.928	1.933	1.828	1.697
Minimum	1.000	1.000	1.000	1.000	1.000
Maximum	16.000	14.000	12.000	12.000	11.000
Number of non-executive directors					
Mean	2.400	2.504	2.604	2.707	2.747
Median	2.000	2.000	2.000	3.000	3.000
Standard deviation	1.690	1.648	1.653	1.689	1.486
Minimum	0.000	0.000	0.000	0.000	0.000
Maximum	9.000	8.000	10.000	10.000	7.000
Executive directors as a percentage of total board					
Mean	69.0	68.3	66.4	64.9	63.3
Median	66.7	66.7	66.7	66.7	61.5
Standard deviation	18.8	17.6	17.2	18.0	15.7
Minimum	11.1	12.5	10.0	9.1	12.5
Maximum	100.0	100.0	100.0	100.0	100.0

seven board members throughout the period. However, in 1988, the average board was composed of approximately five executive directors and two non-executive directors, whereas by 1992, it was composed of approximately four executive directors and three non-executive directors.

Table 1.4 offers univariate statistics for the performance variables. The market value to equity ratio exhibited a mean value of 1.86 and the mean return on shareholders' equity (profits scaled by the book value of equity) was 13%. Turning to operating profit scaled by total assets, the sample had a mean value of approximately 9% with a range from −15% to 24%. Equally, when the average change in market value across the period is considered, there is a range from 3% to 322% with a mean of 79%. Finally, shareholders market return averaged 86%, which reflects the general bull nature of the market across the period.

The second part of Table 1.4 offers univariate statistics for the control variables. The mean level of sales for the period was £409 million with a highly skewed range from £10 million to £485 million. Somewhat surprisingly, given the random nature of the sample, the average Beta is 0.94, which tends to suggest that the systematic risk of the sample is less than the market portfolio. Not surprisingly, however, given the period under consideration, sales growth (*GROWTH*) was, on average, negative. The sample also displayed a limited degree of diversification (a mean level of 75% with 100% signifying no diversification). Of the remaining control variables, the 50% average figure for the *DEBT* variable and its great range should be noted. The bottom section of the table indicates a reasonable spread across eight sectors with a predominance in the building and construction, and engineering and electronic sectors.

(d) Multivariate Results

The empirical analysis consists of a series of Halbert White corrected OLS regressions. The preliminary regression analysis of the relationship between the performance variables and the explanatory variables is presented in Table 1.5. In all performance equations the coefficient on the variables representing the percentage of shares held by institutions (*INSTPER*) is insignificant. Furthermore, replacing *INSTPER* with the dummy variable *INSTDUM* provided similar results. In addition, with the exception of the *RSEREM* equation in which *DIR* is positive and significant only at the 10% confidence level, there is no evidence to suggest that directors' shareholdings or other ownership interests have any impact on the performance of the firm. However, there is evidence to suggest the

Table 1.4   Performance and Control Variables: Summary Statistics

	Mean	Median	Standard deviation	Minimum	Maximum
Performance variables					
Market value/ equity	1.86	1.60	1.26	0.44	10.67
Return on shareholders' equity	0.13	0.13	0.10	−0.21	0.38
Return on shareholders' equity before directors remuneration	0.15	0.14	0.10	−0.14	0.47
Operating profit/total assets	0.092	0.092	0.054	−0.154	0.244
Change in market value	0.794	0.674	0.537	0.026	3.222
Shareholders' return	0.861	0.787	0.525	0.074	2.567
Control variables					
Sales	408870.40	98817.42	821350.90	10429.81	4847875.62
Beta	0.940	0.960	0.219	0.230	1.490
Growth	−0.034	−0.067	0.385	−0.944	2.044
Divers	0.745	0.819	0.251	0.250	1.000
Fasales	0.371	0.229	0.447	0.021	3.108
Rdsales	0.006	0.000	0.017	0.000	0.141
Debt	0.481	0.388	0.509	0.000	5.539

Industry group	Number of firms
Building and Construction	42
Engineering and Electronics	62
Paper and Printing	28
Chemicals	12
Leisure	10
Retailing	40
Breweries	20
Support Services	11

Note: all variables are shown in their unlogged form.

board structure has a significant effect on accounting performance. The variable *BOARD* is positive and significant at the 5% confidence level in all the accounting performance regressions. This therefore suggests that

Table 1.5 OLS Regression Analysis of Performance

Dependent variable	RSE	RSEREM	OPROFTA	VAL	SHRET	CHANGEMV
C	-0.189066	-0.085062	-0.015685	-0.605882	-1.910024	-1.037106
	-1.984445a	-0.793018	-0.359941	-1.280160	-3.255595a	-1.810768b
BETA	0.021103	0.020340	-0.004928	0.126007	-0.594201	-0.290685
	0.726832	0.639533	-0.331237	0.726830	-2.871971a	-1.561064
SIZE	0.025012	0.016992	0.008239	0.084342	0.221203	0.128350
	4.121206a	2.505441a	2.958737a	2.935763a	5.783619a	3.668530a
GROWTH	0.072602	0.081439	0.030907	0.554937	0.285522	0.641597
	3.376149a	3.515673a	2.465890a	6.766099a	2.287825a	5.087001a
DIVERS	-0.001193	-0.007251	0.006207	0.141736	0.082148	-0.046700
	-0.045345	-0.233656	0.438159	0.921495	0.513064	-0.283911
FASALES	-0.034446	-0.048450	-0.009459	-0.270352	-0.075001	-0.151755
	-3.011019a	-4.018329a	-1.618346	-3.799648a	-0.923322	-1.309096
RDSALES	0.365086	0.359965	0.644148	7.187643	2.208891	-0.367085
	1.035125	1.029692	4.127987a	3.513792a	2.932326	-0.352784
BOARD	0.069006	0.089915	0.040470	0.263475	0.997126	-0.261149
	2.076968a	2.516753a	2.135309a	1.326015	1.242806	-0.078635
INDDUM1	-0.068962	-0.070354	-0.011471	-0.410161	-0.532599	-1.066506
	-2.387329a	-2.301350a	-0.719544	-2.390973a	-2.653134a	-1.353739
INDDUM2	-0.028816	-0.026780	-0.012934	-0.381894	-0.298044	-0.286674
	-1.142835	-1.065186	-1.117955	-2.409838a	1.547616	-1.178912

INDDUM3	−0.017817	−0.018082	−0.002708	−0.322790	−0.130604	0.159997
	−0.620330	−0.601368	−0.192401	−1.802420[b]	−0.605609	0.579513
INDDUM4	0.008740	0.009385	−0.009486	−0.212249	−0.168144	−0.019600
	0.256319	0.272153	−0.587220	−1.036690	−0.711447	−0.071153
INDDUM5	−0.049553	−0.045632	−0.024059	−0.269775	−0.273090	−0.245916
	−1.855019[b]	−1.722924[b]	−1.783041[b]	−1.267695	−1.334026	−0.777250
INDDUM6	−0.046597	−0.044060	−0.005244	−0.280064	−0.454641	−0.236880
	−1.696293[b]	−1.602895	−0.393323	−1.620948	−2.206376[a]	−0.955662
INDDUM7	−0.067227	−0.067374	−0.015979	−0.491129	−0.389915	−0.135842
	−2.673470[a]	−2.581525[a]	−1.264032	−2.450605[a]	−2.033279[a]	−0.493841
DEBT	−0.014784	−0.003544	−0.028467	0.124556	−0.502803	−0.513268
	−0.897891	−0.204553	−4.291200[a]	2.278493[a]	−3.148962[a]	−5.801227[a]
DIR	0.000727	0.000948	0.000278	−0.000556	0.004481	0.002744
	1.442870	1.732152[b]	1.033193	−0.201434	1.370786	0.825270
INSTPER	0.001023	0.000989	0.000721	0.001890	0.005043	0.001878
	1.118139	1.008773	1.610972	0.486826	1.081665	0.371490
RELATED	−0.000810	−0.000918	−0.001319	−0.006443	−0.002595	−0.001785
	−0.678647	−0.762204	−1.336540	−1.056353	−0.398261	−0.280341
EXTERNAL	0.000158	5.60E-05	0.000170	0.003387	0.002053	0.000134
	0.329740	0.111841	0.617320	1.146274	0.852073	0.053622
R^2	0.251206	0.224180	0.239794	0.340131	0.374236	0.348745
F-Statistic	4.955135[a]	4.406680[a]	4.718794[a]	7.076912[a]	8.019184[a]	7.313232[a]

[a]Significant at 5% level of confidence.
[b]Significant at 10% level of confidence.
Figures shown are coefficient estimates and *t*-statistics.

the greater the number of executive directors on the board, the better the accounting performance of the firm.

The lack of a significant relationship between directors' shareholdings and performance warrants further examination, particularly in light of the work by Morck, Shleifer and Vishney (1988) and McConnell and Servaes (1990) which suggests that a non-linear relationship exists between performance and directors' shareholdings. Therefore, the performance equations were refined to allow for the possibility that a non-linear relationship provides a better description of the relationship. Morck, Schleifer and Vishney (1988) employed piecewise regression techniques to allow the coefficients on the directors' shareholdings variables to change at the 5% and 25% ownership levels. Their results suggested that a positive relationship exists between performance and directors' owner-ship in the 0–5% ownership range, a negative and less pronounced relationship in the 5–25% range, and a positive but less pronounced relationship beyond the 25% ownership level. In contrast, McConnell and Servaes (1990) found evidence to suggest that the relationship between performance and directors' ownership was curvilinear; performance at first increasing as directors' ownership increased and then decreasing as directors' ownership further increased. However, additional analysis of the relationship between performance and directors' ownership in line with Morck, Schleifer and Vishney, and McConnell and Servaes found little support of a non-linear relationship between performance and directors' ownership.

Therefore overall the results of the first stage of the analysis suggest that institutional shareholdings have little independent effect on the performance of the firm. However, rather than directly affecting firm performance, institutional shareholders may act to curb management discretion by affecting any relationship between directors' shareholdings and firm performance. In order to test this hypothesis, the following variables are defined:

$DIRINST = DIR$ if an individual institutional shareholding is larger than DIR
$DIRNOINST = DIR$ if no individual institutional shareholding is larger than DIR.

If institutions are more capable of monitoring and controlling directors' actions when their shareholding is larger than the directors, it is expected that the coefficient on the variables $DIRINST$ will be larger than on the variable $DIRNOINST$.

Table 1.6 presents the results of the analysis utilising the variables $DIRINST$ and $DIRNOINST$. Only the results of the accounting perform-ance models are reported, the relevant variables were not significant in the

Table 1.6 Effect of Large Institutional Shareholders on Directors' Incentives

Dependent variable	RSE	RSEREM	OPROFTA
C	−0.182607	−0.080066	−0.004149
	−2.220416[a]	−0.880718	−0.098803
BETA	0.021704	0.021182	−0.005977
	0.729901	0.655503	−0.416067
SIZE	0.025170	0.017227	0.007888
	4.592057[a]	2.859675[a]	2.807867[a]
GROWTH	0.071993	0.080870	0.030369
	3.539874[a]	3.655026[a]	2.612042[a]
DIVERS	0.000221	−0.005832	0.006911
	0.008952	−0.196007	0.521254
FASALES	−0.036195	−0.050176	−0.010481
	−3.346181[a]	−4.408606[a]	−1.856284[b]
RDSALES	0.342176	0.336962	0.632867
	0.999905	0.994998	4.306919[a]
BOARD	0.058466	0.079423	0.034773
	1.725029[b]	2.170047[a]	1.831337[b]
INDDUM1	−0.072069	−0.073481	−0.012963
	−2.565455[a]	−2.465290[a]	−0.835777
INDDUM2	−0.027161	−0.025184	−0.011750
	−1.111838	−1.032143	−1.068684
INDDUM3	−0.013386	−0.013699	−0.000158
	−0.483483	−0.471374	−0.011488
INDDUM4	0.011085	0.011683	−0.008017
	0.336879	0.351358	−0.519641
INDDUM5	−0.054932	−0.050894	−0.027487
	−2.081049[a]	−1.930138[b]	−2.146360[a]
INDDUM6	−0.047916	−0.045393	−0.005842
	−1.761170[b]	−1.667248[b]	−0.442749
INDDUM7	−0.071851	−0.071962	−0.018559
	−2.909998[a]	−2.817687[a]	−1.546312
DEBT	−0.016731	−0.005449	−0.029704
	−1.045276	−0.324884	−4.496575[a]
DIRINST	0.009273	0.009430	0.005042
	2.787506[a]	2.619297[a]	2.363613[a]
DIRNOINST	0.000896	0.001120	0.000347
	1.726416[b]	2.008326[a]	1.240496
RELATED	−0.001278	−0.001378	−0.001601
	−1.327544	−1.415965	1.689000[b]
EXTERNAL	0.000193	0.000093	0.000176
	0.424861	0.195601	0.699414
R^2	0.275063	0.246041	0.259629
F-Statistic	5.473278[a]	4.847278[a]	5.134255[a]
F-Statistic for difference between DIRINST and			
DIRNOINST	7.347511[a]	6.151978[a]	5.442067[a]

[a,b] As in Table 1.5.   Figures shown are coefficient estimates and t-statistics.

market performance models. For the accounting performance models, the coefficients on the variables *DIRINST* and *DIRNOINST* are both positive and significant and the coefficient on the variable *DIRINST* is larger than that on the variable *DIRNOINST*. Furthermore, a Wald test confirms that there is a significant difference between these two coefficients. Therefore, there is some evidence to support the hypothesis that the relationship between directors' ownership and performance is affected by the presence of institutional shareholders. Furthermore, the affect of the presence of institutional shareholders would tend to support the monitoring hypothesis, in that the positive relationship between performance and directors' ownership is strengthened in the presence of large institutional shareholders.

The results so far suggest that institutions do not have an independent effect on performance, but rather that they act to curb directors' discretion by affecting the relationship between directors' ownership and performance. However, the relationship between firm performance and institutional ownership may be dependent on the percentage of shares held by other large external shareholders (e.g. individuals and companies). Other large external shareholders may be expected to be less diversified than institutional investors and hence have more incentives to monitor management actions. Hence, in the presence of such external shareholders, institutions may be able to take more of a 'back seat'. If this is the case, the relationship between firm performance and institutional shareholdings should be stronger when no other external shareholders are present.

To test this hypothesis, the following variables are defined:

LGINST = percentage of shares held by institutions (*INSTPER*) if other large external shareholders owning 5% or more are present, 0 otherwise.
NOLGINST = *INSTPER* if no other large external shareholders owning 5% or more is present, 0 otherwise.

Table 1.7 presents the results of the regression models using the variables *LGINST* and *NOLGINST* in place of institutional shareholdings and other

Table 1.7   Interaction Between Institutions and Other External Shareholders

Dependent variable	RSE	RSEREM	OPROFTA
C	−0.200529	−0.098858	−0.015231
	−2.180223[a]	−0.972322	−0.349765
BETA	0.007815	0.009050	−0.007413
	0.268314	0.279106	−0.517234

Table 1.7 (*continued*)

Dependent variable	*RSE*	*RSEREM*	*OPROFTA*
SIZE	0.026970	0.018908	0.008293
	4.463033[a]	2.895565[a]	2.826167[a]
GROWTH	0.076322	0.085188	0.031878
	4.234082[a]	4.283698[a]	2.717445[a]
DIVERS	−0.013968	−0.019270	0.004639
	−0.548532	−0.624394	0.338932
FASALES	−0.040813	−0.054240	−0.010625
	−3.926804[a]	−4.907366[a]	−1.852733[b]
RDSALES	0.325355	0.300433	0.669849
	1.047489	0.964832	4.210975[a]
BOARD	0.040578	0.060975	0.033345
	1.245246	1.761203[b]	1.700647[b]
INDDUM1	−0.051037	−0.052495	−0.006520
	−1.871922[b]	−1.808198[b]	−0.439293
INDDUM2	−0.014471	−0.012062	−0.009557
	−0.571427	−0.476103	−0.829570
INDDUM3	−0.013286	−0.012605	0.000507
	−0.460407	−0.413618	0.036862
INDDUM4	0.040907	0.041510	0.000904
	1.212781	1.238366	0.055294
INDDUM5	−0.025204	−0.021024	−0.017438
	−0.864933	−0.720020	−1.290000
INDDUM6	−0.035289	−0.032839	0.001407
	−1.280473	−1.194518	−0.105556
INDDUM7	−0.047777	−0.047692	−0.010003
	−1.914246[b]	−1.838022[b]	−0.803910
DEBT	−0.012597	−0.001070	−0.026934
	−0.818137	−0.064986	−3.907149[a]
DIR0−5	0.011060	0.011180	0.003433
	2.889760[a]	2.750899[a]	1.630181
DIR5−25	−0.000568	−0.000527	−0.000772
	−0.512159	−0.416018	−1.270548
DIR25+	−0.000118	0.000346	0.000677
	−0.094958	0.242714	1.114755
LGINST	−0.001280	−0.001410	0.000257
	−0.909366	−0.960659	0.346420
NOLGINST	0.001913	0.001956	0.000912
	2.391020[a]	2.315370[a]	1.904913[b]
RELATED	−0.001070	−0.001107	−0.001229
	−1.003139	−1.024373	−1.297294
R^2	0.302847	0.272139	0.243100
F-Statistic	5.633649[a]	4.988149[a]	4.425899[a]

[a,b] As in Table 1.5.
Figures shown are coefficient estimates and *t*-statistics.

external shareholdings. Once again, for the market-based models, the coefficients are insignificant and hence the models are not presented. However, for the accounting-based models, the coefficient on the variable *NOLGINST* is positive and significant, while that on the variable *LGINST* is insignificant. These results therefore suggest that the percentage of shares held by institutions has a significantly positive effect on performance only when there are no other large external shareholders. Hence this suggests that, where possible, institutions rely on other large external shareholders to provide the monitoring, which is not surprising, given the size of institutions' portfolios. Again, it needs to be noted, that the influence of ownership variables is primarily felt with accounting measures of performance and not market-based measures.

In summary, the results of the present analysis would seem to indicate that the relationship between corporate performance and institutional shareholdings is complex and is affected by interactions with other shareholding parties. When considered independently of other ownership interests, there would appear to be no significant relationship between performance and institutional ownership. However, the results do suggest that the presence of institutional shareholders acts to curb management discretion by strengthening the positive relationship between performance and directors' ownership. This result is consistent with that of McConnell and Servaes (1990, 1995). Furthermore, there appears to be an interaction between institutional shareholders and other external shareholders, in that institutional shareholdings have a significantly positive effect on performance, only in the absence of other large external shareholders.

All the above conclusions are mainly derived for accounting measures of performance. In general, the ownership variables have little impact on market-based measures of performance. The conclusion to be drawn from such a mixture of results is that although greater alignment of ownership and control has a positive impact on short-term profits, the market has not yet positively reacted to the changes. Indeed, the impact of the ownership variables on accounting measures of performance is relatively small compared to the effects of size and growth. One interpretation of these joint results, therefore, is perhaps it is not surprising that the ownership effects are swamped in market assessments of actual and expected corporate performance. Alternatively, concentrated ownership may have an adverse effect on market performance, as it restricts the liquidity of the shares in issue. Another interpretation, however, is that the market perceives the accounting measures of performance to be open to manipulation by directors and accordingly discounts their value. Which interpretation is correct awaits further investigation.

Furthermore, empirical problems exist in attempting to model the relationship between institutional ownership and firm performance; for example, much research is constrained by the use of publicly available data on institutional ownership.[3] In addition, by focusing on the presence of institutional shareholders and/or the percentage of shares owned by institutions, there is an inherent assumption that a certain level of institutional shareholding is associated with a certain level of monitoring activity.

CONCLUSIONS

The arguments reviewed in this chapter suggest that from an economic rationality perspective there are good reasons for an individual institution not to become involved in the governance of corporations. Nonetheless, the process of life within the Square Mile may help to overcome the direct disincentives from private action on the part of the institutions. In essence, the theoretical arguments do not give a positive guide as to the impact of institutions on corporate governance. The empirical results presented here, however, suggest that institutional shareholders do have an effect on corporate performance, albeit a rather complex one.

Having found some empirical support for corporate performance being influenced by institutional investors, there is now a need to interpret such a result in the general context of the UK financial system. On the face of it, the result regarding performance contradicts the rationality argument which suggests that individual institutions should not become involved in corporate governance issues. As noted, however, the rationality arguments do not take into account the institutional framework of the Square Mile that has evolved over a number of centuries. The institutional investors in the UK form a highly concentrated network, often operating in the confines of the Square Mile with a well-developed history of relationships and communication. This facilitates the operation of club-like dynamics and the possibility of concerted/focused action. Furthermore, this network of institutions operates within a society with strong laws of libel and slander, and a general preference for action behind the scenes. In this form of society, it may, of course, be extremely difficult to directly identify actions that could be definitely categorised under the banner of governance; actions taking place through gentle persuasion and the knowledge that the potential public disclosure of opinions can be extremely damaging. In fact, the tendency to work behind closed doors in the UK reinforces the strength of any potential threat to 'go public'. Such a threat, of course, is only likely to be credible if the companies believe it is in the interests of the institutions to voice their concerns publicly. It is clear, however, that the nature of governance within the UK is such that it is difficult to determine visibly how far it is in operation. Nonetheless, the overall effect from such a network of activities should be a positive correlation between the presence of institutions and the performance of individual corporations. In response to this, the present analysis concludes that the presence of institutional shareholders does have a positive effect on corporate performance by affecting the relationship between performance and other ownership interests.

NOTES

1. Black and Coffee (1994) report that Prudential Portfolio Managers Ltd, the investment subsidiary of the Prudential, own a stake of 5% or higher in about 200 companies, but become concerned about illiquidity at ownership stakes in the region of 10%. However, the Prudential is the UK's single largest institutional investor, owning over 3% of the stock market. Smaller institutions would clearly be required to take smaller stakes in the larger companies in order to maintain liquidity.
2. This reflects a style of regulation which is firmly within the tradition of 'British policy style' which emphasises consultation, persuasion, co-operation and accommodation between 'reasonable people' rather than compulsion and conflict. See Jordan and Richardson (1982) for a discussion of this style of negotiation.
3. In the UK, companies have to disclose external ownership interests amounting to 3% or more (5% or more prior to 1990) in their Annual Report. While a complete record of shareholders' equity interests can be obtained from a company's register, problems associated with processing such a large amount of data normally prohibit its use. However, in very recent times, commercial organisations are producing shareholder lists on CD-ROM, detailing ownership interests in excess of, for example, 0.25%.

REFERENCES

Black, B.S. and Coffee, J.C. (1994) Hail Britannia? Institutional investor behaviour under limited regulation. *Michigan Law Review*, **92**, 7, 1997–2087.

Blake, D. (1992) *Issues in Pension Funding*, London: Routledge.

Brickley, J.A., Lease, R.C. and Smith, C.W. (1988) Ownership structure and voting on antitakeover amendments. *Journal of Financial Economics*, **20**, 267–91.

Brickley, J.A., Lease, R.C. and Smith, C.W. (1994) Corporate voting: evidence from charter amendment proposals. *Journal of Corporate Finance*, **1**, 5–31.

Cadbury, A. (1990) Owners and investors. In *Creative Tension?* London: National Association of Pension Funds.

Cadbury, A. (1992) *Report on the Committee on the Financial Aspects of Corporate Governance*, London: Gee and Co.

Central Statistical Office (1994a) *Share Register Survey Report End 1993*, London: HMSO.

Central Statistical Office (1994b) *Financial Statistics*, August, London: HMSO.

Chaganti R. and Damanpur, F. (1991) Institutional ownership, capital structure and firm performance. *Strategic Management Journal*, **12**, 479–91.

Charkham, J.P. (1990) Are shares just commodities? In *Creative Tension?* London: National Association of Pension Funds, pp. 34–42.

Coffee, J.C. (1991) Liquidity versus control: the institutional investor as corporate monitor. *Columbia Law Review*, **91**, 6, 1277–1368.

Denis, D.J. and Denis, D.K. (1994) Majority owner–managers and organisational efficiency. *Journal of Corporate Finance*, **1**, 91–118.

Drucker, P.F. (1976) *The Unseen Revolution; How Pension Fund Socialism Came to America*, London: Heinemann.

Fama, E.F. (1980) Agency problems and the theory of the firm. *Journal of Political Economy*, **88**, 288 307.

Grossman, S. and Hart, O. (1982) Corporate financial structure and managerial incentives. In McCall, J. (ed.), *The Economics of Information and Uncertainty*, Chicago: University of Chicago Press, pp. 107–37.

Hermalin, B.E. and Weisbach, M.S. (1988) The determinants of board composition. *Rand Journal of Economics*, **19**, 4, 589–606.

Hermalin, B.E. and Weisbach, M.S. (1991) The effects of board composition and direct incentives on firm performance. *Financial Management*, Winter, 101–12.

Hirschman, A.O. (1970) *Exit, Voice and Loyalty: Responses to Decline in Firms, Organisations and States*, Cambridge, MA: Harvard University Press.

Holderness, C.G. and Sheehan, D.P. (1988) The role of majority shareholders in publicly held corporations: an exploratory analysis. *Journal of Financial Economics*, **20**, 317–46.

Holland, J. (1994) Corporate governance and financial institutions. Unpublished Working Paper, University of Glasgow.

Hutton, W. (1995) *The State We're In*, London: Jonathan Cape.

Jenkinson, T. and Mayer, C. (1992) The assessment: corporate governance and corporate control. *Oxford Review of Economic Policy*, **8**, 3, 1–10.

Jensen, M.C. and Meckling, W.H. (1976) Theory of the firm: managerial behaviour, agency costs and ownership structure, *Journal of Financial Economics*, **4**, 305–60.

Jensen, M.C. (1986) Agency costs of free cash flow, corporate finance and takeovers. *American Economic Review,* **76**, 323–9.

Jordan, G. and Richardson, J. (1982) The British policy style or the logic of negotiation? In Richardson, J. (ed.), *Policy Styles in Western Europe,* London: George Allen and Unwin.

Leech, D. and Leahy, J. (1991) Ownership structure, control type classifications and the performance of large British companies. *Economic Journal,* **101**, 1418–37.

McConnell, J. J. and Servaes, H. (1990) Additional evidence on equity ownership and corporate value. *Journal of Financial Economics,* **27**, 595–612.

McConnell, J.J. and Servaes, H. (1995) Equity ownership and the two faces of debt. *Journal of Financial Economics,* **39**, 131–57.

Morck, R., Shleifer, A. and Vishney, R.W. (1988) Management ownership and market valuation: an empirical analysis. *Journal of Financial Economics,* **20**, 293–315.

Murali, R. and Welch, J.B. (1989) Agents, owners, control and performance. *Journal of Business Finance and Accounting,* Summer, 385–98.

Pearce, J.A. and Zahra, S.A. (1992) Board composition from a strategic contingency perspective. *Journal of Management Studies,* **29**, 4, 411–38.

Pound, J. (1988) Proxy contests and the efficiency of shareholder oversight. *Journal of Financial Economics,* **20**, 237–65.

Rosenstein, S. and Wyatt, J.G. (1990) Outside directors, board independence and shareholder wealth. *Journal of Financial Economics,* **26**, 175–91.

Short, H. (1994) Ownership, control, financial structure and the performance of firms. *Journal of Economic Surveys,* **8**, 3, 203–49.

Short, H. and Keasey, K. (1995) Institutional shareholders and corporate governance in the UK: arguments and evidence. Report for the Research Board of the Institute of Chartered Accountants of England and Wales.

Stiglitz, J.E. (1985) Credit markets and the control of capital. *Journal of Money, Credit and Banking,* **17**, 2, 133–52.

Weisbach, M.S. (1988) Outside directors and CEO turnover. *Journal of Financial Economics,* **20**, 431–60.

Zeckhauser R.I. and Pound, J. (1990) Are large shareholders effective monitors? An investigation of share ownership and corporate performance. In Hubbard, R.G. (ed.), *Asymmetric Information, Corporate Finance and Investment,* Chicago: University of Chicago Press.

——— 2 ———
Executive Remuneration and Corporate Performance

MAHMOUD EZZAMEL and ROBERT WATSON

INTRODUCTION

The potential conflict of interest between owners and managers has been extensively discussed in the literature, particularly since the seminal work of Berle and Means (1932) and as the management-controlled form with diffused ownership has progressively become the dominant organisational form in North America and the UK. Investigations into the (possible and actual) economic consequences of such conflict of interest, and the extent to which the interests of shareholders and management can be better aligned by various organisational, contractual and incentive mechanisms, has been the main focus of academic research over recent years.

Typically, in widely held firms, while owners provide the risk capital, it is the professional executives who are responsible for making strategic and operational decisions which internally allocate and deploy these resources. This in itself does not pose a serious problem if shareholders are able to monitor managers easily and cheaply and make them accountable for their actions. The problem of accountability generally arises because the executives will normally have a distinct information advantage over diffused owners that the latter cannot overcome at low cost. Generally, information asymmetries can be expected to persist since it is difficult for shareholders to obtain unbiased information at low cost due

Corporate Governance: Responsibilities, Risks and Remuneration. Edited by Kevin Keasey and Mike Wright © 1997 John Wiley & Sons Ltd.

to executives' control over the reporting of internal information and their possession of firm and industry-specific knowledge/skills not shared by owners or other external market analysts. Hence, managers are able to exploit such information asymmetries to pursue goals which could be different from those of owners and/or be detrimental to their economic interests. The economics-based literature has identified this conflict of interest between owners and managers as presenting an 'agency cost' problem with the twin dimensions of adverse selection (*ex ante* opportunism) and moral hazard (*ex post* opportunism).

A number of researchers have explored various means by which agency costs may be minimised. These include Jensen and Meckling's (1976) suggestion to use monitoring and bonding arrangements and Fama and Jensen's (1983a,b) proposal that decision management (initiation of decisions and implementation of ratified decisions) and decision control (ratification and monitoring of decisions) should be separated and diffused across many agents. In addition, numerous other external and internal monitoring mechanisms have been suggested; these include outside (non-executive) directors, bank lenders (Hirshleiffer and Suh, 1992), professional board members, large institutional shareholders (whether with *or* without board seats), large individual shareholders (including those who act as CEOs *or* those who delegated management to professional CEOs) and the firm's auditors.

In the wake of the economic downturn in the UK after 1990, a spate of unexpected company failures, financial scandals and examples of 'corporate excesses', such as high pay awards to the executives of poorly performing companies threatened to undermine investor confidence in the corporate sector. In an attempt to restore public confidence in the UK corporate sector, a committee of inquiry (the Cadbury Committee) was set up in 1991 by the Stock Exchange and Financial Reporting Council to investigate the financial aspects of corporate governance and to produce proposals which would improve UK corporate governance. The Cadbury Committee, which published its final report in December 1992, envisaged a much greater monitoring role for non-executive directors and recommended a voluntary 'code of best practice' to be implemented, along with a 'statement of compliance' reviewed by the auditors and published with the annual financial accounts, by all listed companies reporting after 30 June 1993. The code included a requirement for companies to have at least three (independent) non-executive directors and the introduction of two new board committees made up of non-executive directors: (1) an audit committee, to create a clearer avenue of communication between auditors and shareholders, and (2) a remuneration committee to determine senior executive pay and to ensure that large pay awards were justified by increases in firm performance and shareholder wealth.

This chapter examines the relationship between the levels and changes in senior executive remuneration and a range of variables measuring important aspects of firm size and performance, job characteristics, human capital, and corporate governance characteristics. In particular, we examine whether post-Cadbury pay awards to senior executives have, as intended, succeeded in creating a stronger link between senior executive pay and performance, or whether executive pay can be explained more adequately by external market comparisons. Our empirical results indicate that changes in executive pay are more closely related to external market comparison pay levels than to changes in either profits or shareholder wealth. Moreover, the results suggest a marked asymmetry in treatment between those executives that appeared to be, relative to market comparison pay levels, under- and overpaid. Executives that appeared to be underpaid in 1992, given their firm size and performance, experienced a large and highly significant upward adjustment in their pay in the following year while no comparable downward adjustment in the size of pay awards was apparent in the case of seemingly overpaid executives. These results are consistent with the complaints of shareholder groups that remuneration committees simply result in bidding up executive pay rather than making pay any more dependent upon performance.

The remainder of the chapter is organised as follows. In the next section we provide an overview of previous literature on executive remuneration and firm performance and briefly describe some of the recent developments in corporate governance in the UK. This is followed by a description of our research method, the models adopted for empirical analysis, and the sample and data selection. We then present and discuss our empirical results prior to summarising our main findings and discussing their implications in the concluding section.

EXECUTIVE REMUNERATION, FIRM PERFORMANCE AND CORPORATE GOVERNANCE: PREVIOUS RESEARCH

In this section we provide a brief overview of previous studies, both theoretical and empirical, on executive remuneration before we describe the recent UK experience with corporate governance.

Executive Remuneration and Firm Performance: Theory and Evidence

The vast majority of studies that have examined the relationship between senior executive remuneration and firm performance have adopted an agency theory perspective and have concentrated upon the presumed incentive and control aspects of the relationship (see Roson, 1990; Main, 1991; Pavlik, Scott and Tiessen, 1993 for reviews).[1] As Jensen and Meckling (1976) and Fama and Jensen (1983a,b) have suggested, within the context of agency theory, the writing of employment contracts is an important means by which the principal (shareholders and/or their representatives, non-executive directors) can control the activities of the agent (senior management). Clearly, a prominent feature of such contracts would be clauses relating to the performance and incentive compensation of the agent. Managerial compensation is, however, typically made up of base salary, cash bonuses, and stock options but may also include various fringe benefits and other perquisites. In practice, cash bonuses are usually based on current firm accounting earnings and/or stock market returns and, hence, are largely rewards for relatively short-term performance, whilst share options are generally considered to provide longer-term financial incentives for executives to act in shareholder interests.

Within an agency theory perspective, where it is usually assumed that the principal is either risk-neutral or risk-averse and the agent is assumed to be both risk- and effort-averse, contracts have both insurance and incentive effects. In situations where the agent's efforts and output are observable the principal can eliminate shirking by the agent through monitoring (Holmstrom, 1979) and the agent's compensation will be a flat wage (irrespective of the level of output). However, when output is observable but the agent's effort is unobservable (or when random factors affect output) Holmstrom has shown that the agent's reward should be contingent on the output obtained in order to provide an incentive for the agent to exert greater effort to increase output. This clearly establishes a strong link between firm performance and executive compensation. The precise relationship between the agent's effort and output determines the relative importance of the incentive and insurance dimensions of the contract. As the principal can infer more information about the agent's effort from the output, the agent's compensation becomes more reliant on output and hence the insurance that the principal offers the agent becomes smaller. Any additional signals (i.e. other than output) that allow the principal to infer more information on the agent's effort should be incorporated into the contract because of its informational content (Bankar and Datar, 1989).

The important conclusion to emerge from the above discussion is that in the more common case of both the principal and the agent being risk-averse, optimal risk sharing necessitates that at least part of the agent's reward is made contingent on output. Note, however, that agency theory's conception of the determinants of an executive's base salary (the insurance aspect) is fairly limited, that is, it is viewed as largely a function of the ease or otherwise experienced by the principal in monitoring executive behaviour and/or output. Nevertheless, the simple requirement of firms to retain and attract suitably qualified individuals for executive posts suggests that an undeniably important influence upon the minimum level of base salaries will be external labour market constraints based upon comparisons with the pay levels of similar executives in similar sized firms. Consideration of these external labour market factors suggests, therefore, that changes in base salaries are likely to be more closely related to salary levels external to the firm than to firm-specific performance measures.[2]

A growing body of empirical evidence on executive compensation and its relationship to firm performance is gradually emerging in the literature; but there are some controversies and puzzling departures from the theoretical rationalisation of performance-based rewards in agency theory. For example, Benson (1985) has argued that compensation schemes used in practice, particularly those focusing on the proportion of CEOs' personal wealth that is linked to the fortunes of the firm (rather than cash compensation), provide a sufficient incentive to align the interests of managers to those of the owners. In contrast, Jensen and Murphy (1990) observe only a very weak link between compensation and firm performance: changes in shareholders wealth were found to explain only 2% of the CEO cash compensation and 3% of the CEO total compensation.

To gain a more informed understanding of the relationship between executive compensation and performance we need to examine more closely some of the earlier empirical work. From the 1960s onwards a number of studies tested empirically Baumol's (1967) sales-maximisation hypothesis which states that when ownership is divorced from control managers tend to pursue their own goals (e.g. sales maximisation) rather than those of the owners. These studies (e.g. Lewellen and Huntsman, 1970; Cosh, 1975; Ciscel and Carroll, 1980) found that cash compensation was positively associated with sales and, to a lesser extent, accounting profit. Other researchers sought to address some of the limitations identified in these previous studies by incorporating additional measures of corporate performance such as share performance and by broadening the definition of compensation beyond cash. For example, Masson (1971) reported a strong association between comprehensive compensation and share performance which dominated the sales and accounting profit measures; a finding which is contrary to the sales-maximisation hypothesis presumed to be supported by the earlier studies. Subsequent studies, while refining and improving upon the research method used by Masson, supported his conclusions (e.g. Murphy, 1985; Antle and Smith, 1986; Jensen and Murphy, 1990; Clinch, 1991). Moreover, Benson (1985) and Murphy (1985) reported that when firms experience large share returns, the changes in executives' wealth from holding shares are very large relative to their salaries, thereby implying that executives are likely to be concerned with the behaviour of share returns.

Moreover, while the initial results of some researchers (e.g. Murphy, 1985; Coughlan and Schmidt, 1985) show a positive association between executive compensation and sales growth (the latter being a proxy for firm size), refinements in their research methodology (e.g. Barro and Barro, 1990; Jensen and Murphy, 1990) revealed that sales growth was significant only when accounting return and security return were not included in the explanatory variables. However, it should be noted that despite such modifications in the results, executives' *initial* compensation remains strongly associated with firm size, thereby suggesting that larger, more complex firms recruit more highly paid executives.

A number of recent UK studies (Conyon and Leech, 1994; Gregg, Machin and Szymanski, 1993; Ogden and Watson, 1996) have also examined the relationship between changes in executive pay and firm performance and have found little evidence of an economically significant relationship once firm size measures are included in the estimating equation.[3] Clearly, since incentive-based pay is only necessary in order to mitigate monitoring and agency problems, the institutional mechanisms by which executive pay is set, i.e. corporate governance characteristics, should be important factors in explaining the relative strength of any pay–firm performance relationship. However, *a priori*, it is unclear which corporate governance characteristics will be the most appropriate measures for examining the relationship between pay and firm performance. Moreover, because governance mechanisms may complement and/ or be cheaper substitutes for other control mechanisms such as performance-based bonuses, share option awards, etc., it is also unclear whether empirically the link will necessarily be stronger when executives are adequately monitored and accountable to shareholders.[4] For instance, if corporate governance arrangements simply allow executives freedom to set their own pay, then a stronger pay–firm performance link might be observed during a period of rising profits than for firms where significant shareholders and/or non-executive directors are able to control executives more directly. In this context, the Conyon and Leech (1994) study is particularly interesting since it also examined the influence of corporate governance variables upon executive pay awards. What they found, however, was that

> 'whilst ownership control and concentration depress the level of director pay in the sample period, these variables have no effect on the growth in directors' pay. Moreover, separating the role of chairman and chief executive, or where the major shareholders are insurance companies, has no effect on the level or growth in directors' pay' (p. 230).

We now turn our attention to the system of corporate governance in the UK and the proposals of the Cadbury Committee report (1992), which envisaged making executive pay awards more accountable via the setting up of remuneration committees made up of independent non-executive directors.

Corporate Governance in the UK

Formally, corporate governance in the UK provides for a chain of accountability whereby executives are accountable to the board of directors, who are in turn accountable to the shareholders. This structure is intended to improve executives' accountability while allowing them to manage the firm without having shareholders directly interfering in its day-to-day operations. However, in practice the distinction between managers (accountable to the board) and directors (accountable to shareholders) is less than obvious because the boards of most large publicly quoted firms are dominated by executive directors (e.g. Cosh and Hughes, 1987; Davis and Kay, 1993; Ezzamel and Watson, 1996). Prima facie, this suggests that the ability of non-executive directors to exert effective control over executives is seriously curtailed. Apart from the right to sell their shares, shareholders' formal powers are largely limited to electing and re-electing the board at the annual general meeting (AGM). Moreover, unless the firm is performing particularly badly, the AGM is normally a perfunctory affair and it is rare for the board to be seriously questioned regarding corporate strategy or be pressured by shareholders into changes of policy or personnel (Morck, Shleifer and Vishney, 1989; Charkham, 1989).

As Forbes and Watson (1993) have suggested, the real problem is not the lack of formal powers of the shareholders but rather of incentives to act and the difficulties in using what powers they have. The incentive problem arises because of the 'public good' characteristics (jointly supply and non-excludability) of monitoring and control activities (Mueller, 1979). Typically, each shareholder has only a tiny proportion of the firm's equity. In the absence of an easily enforceable collective arrangement, it is impossible to exclude 'free riders' from the benefits arising from improved monitoring by an individual shareholder. Benefits, but not costs, will be shared with other 'free-riding' shareholders and, in consequence, the expected benefits accruing to the individual that incurred the full monitoring costs will only be in proportion to his or her equity holdings. As with all public goods, in the absence of collective provision there may be too few resources devoted to ensuring that sufficient monitoring takes place (see Stiglitz, 1985). Moreover, because institutional shareholders have no right in UK law to interfere with management, even if they succeed in removing an executive director from the board, they cannot also strip the executive of his or her executive responsibilities since this power lies solely with the board. The existence of active secondary markets and the difficulties of intervention normally provides such institutional shareholders with the less costly option of simply exiting. In consequence, there is an absence of committed owners that find it in their interests to actively monitor and control managerial actions.

It has been suggested that other external (market) control mechanisms such as the labour market's assessment of an executive's track record and competence (Fama, 1980), the threat of take-over (Jensen, 1986, 1989), debtholder actions (Grossman and Hart, 1982; Wruck, 1990) and monitoring by city analysts may effectively constrain managers from straying too far from shareholder wealth maximisation and/or may provide for the removal of incompetent managers.

However, the efficacy of each of these mechanisms in respect of ensuring managerial accountability is somewhat limited. Clearly, if shareholders are unable to adequately monitor their own agents, then it can be expected that external managerial labour markets will also typically be too informationally imperfect to operate effectively as a powerful sanction against opportunistic and/or poorly performing managers. Debtholders can only intervene when the security of their investment is seriously at risk and therefore only very poorly performing firms or firms experiencing a significant restructuring in ownership such as management buyouts (see Thompson and Wright, 1995, for a review) are likely to be subject to this control mechanism.[5] Financial analysts obtain much of their information from firms they are monitoring and are often rewarded on the basis of the amount of business they generate from clients. Criticisms of a firm's management are likely to sour relations and are unlikely to directly generate new business or bonuses for the analyst. The market for corporate control, while perhaps successful in some instances at removing poor mangers, is no less likely to result in the removal of good managers. Indeed, the possibility of takeover further reduces shareholders' incentives to monitor managers. This is because control of a firm is of value to a bidder and, therefore, the takeover threat provides current shareholders with the possibility of realising a bid premium irrespective of whether or not the bidder will actually improve firm performance. Furthermore, much managerial time and resources are consumed in devising strategies which though they may reduce the threat of takeover often do so in ways that are inconsistent with shareholders' interests (Charkham, 1989).

The UK system of corporate accountability does not require either a supervisory tier or even outside (non-executive) directors on the boards of companies, and hence it is largely dependent upon the self-discipline of executive directors. The perception that self-discipline was failing to ensure managerial accountability led to the setting up of the Cadbury Committee, co-sponsored by the Financial Reporting Council and The Stock Exchange. The Cadbury Committee's draft report *Financial Aspects of Corporate Governance* published in 1992 had as its remit 'the control and reporting functions of boards, and the role of auditors and shareholders'. The Committee proposals rely largely upon continued self-regulation, improved information to shareholders and a strengthening of the independence of auditors. The Committee established a Code of Best Practice for boards of directors which stipulated that:

- All quoted companies should have at least three non-executive directors, directors' service contracts should not exceed three years without shareholders' approval and that the posts of CEO and chairman of the board should not be held by the same individual.
- The total emoluments of directors and those of the chairman and the highest-paid UK director should be fully disclosed and split into their salary and performance-related components and the basis by which the latter is determined should also be explained.

- Executive directors' remuneration should be subject to the recommendations of a remuneration committee made up wholly or mainly of non-executive directors.
- Boards of directors must set up effective audit committees and report on the effectiveness of their system of internal financial control.

The Cadbury proposals rely heavily upon the ability and willingness of non-executive directors to monitor and control effectively the activities of the executives on the board. Clearly, if non-executive directors are to fulfil these monitoring and control functions effectively they need to be independent of management and to possess the power and incentive to act decisively in situations where executives appear not to be acting in shareholder interests. Note, however, that UK company law does not make any distinction between executive and non-executive board members and both groups have identical legal responsibilities. Hence, the independence of non-executive directors is inevitably constrained given that they are legally an integral part of the management team that they are supposed to be monitoring. Moreover, since executives have both a decisive voice in choosing the non-executive board members and also form the majority of members on the boards of UK companies, it is far from clear that non-executive directors possess either the power or incentive to challenge managerial actions.[6] Not surprisingly, several writers have questioned the independence of non-executive directors; for example, Jensen (1989, p. 64) has suggested that the idea that 'outside directors with little or no equity stake in the company could effectively monitor and discipline the managers who selected them has proven hollow at best'.

A number of UK-based studies (Cosh and Hughes, 1987; Main and Johnston, 1992, 1993; IDS, 1993) also suggest that the level of independence of UK non-executive directors is similarly fairly limited. However, a US study by Byrd and Hickman (1992) into the effects on tender offer bids indicated that, in this context at least, shareholders appear to gain from more effective monitoring by independent outside directors, but that these gains may be subject to diminishing returns as the proportion of outside directors on the board went above 60%.

Evidence from both the UK and the USA (where remuneration committees are almost universal) strongly suggests that not only do outside directors typically have close ties with the executive directors they are meant to be monitoring, but that they are also no less likely to award large pay rises which bear little relation to company performance. Studies by Main (1991), Main and Johnston (1993) and O'Reilley, Main and Crystal

(1988) indicate the 'strong social influence considerations' that affect the pay awards granted by remuneration committees. These studies suggest that the remuneration received by non-executive directors in their own companies largely conditions what is deemed to be a 'reasonable' pay award when serving on the remuneration committee of other companies.

A recent UK study by Main and Johnston (1993) indicated that, even after controlling for differences in firm size and performance, the level of pay awarded to chief executives when the firm had a remuneration committee was significantly higher than for firms without such committees. Their estimates suggest that, on average, remuneration committees award an additional 17–21%, or some £56 000 per annum, to their CEOs. However, as the authors point out, the main purpose of a remuneration committee is not to hold down, or for that matter to increase, pay levels, but rather to tie pay more closely to company performance. In this respect Main and Johnston's results regarding the breakdown between pay in cash and pay in the form of stock options, which showed that 'there was no discernible effect that could be attributed to the existence of a remuneration committee' (p. 358), suggests that there was little evidence that at the time of the Cadbury report, remuneration committees in either the UK or the USA were having the desired effect of more closely tying executive pay awards to increases in shareholder wealth.

These empirical findings appear to be consistent with what has already been said regarding the decisive role that external labour market comparisons can be expected to play in regard to changes in executive's base salaries and the fact that the non-executives serving on the remuneration committee also have to work closely with the executives on the board in framing the major strategic plans of the business. Clearly, non-executives have few incentives to risk causing serious offence to the senior executive board members and, therefore, it should not be surprising to learn that remuneration committees generally attempt to shift the responsibility for determining salary levels onto outside pay consultants (see IDS, 1993, for a review). The basing of a large element of executive pay awards largely on the recommendations of outside pay consultants has led to complaints by shareholder groups that this process simply results in 'bidding up' executive pay over time without making pay any more dependent upon firm performance.

The suspicion that a 'cosy collusion' exists between executives and non-executive directors, who are often executives themselves and who sit on each other's remuneration committees and therefore have a common interest in bidding up pay, appears to be widely held (IDS, 1993). For instance, Tatton (1992) of Incomes Data Services (IDS) is on record as stating that 'remuneration committees don't control pay at all, because they are effectively setting their own pay levels. They talk each other up', while the *Financial Times* (20 April 1993) wrote of 'tame non-executive directors sitting on malleable remuneration committees advised by tame pay consultants'. In our empirical analysis of changes in executive pay described below, we attempt to model the bidding up process and test its empirical validity.

THE RESEARCH METHOD

Modelling the Determinants of Executive Pay

The main purpose of this study is to examine empirically the remuneration of senior UK executives (Executive Chairmen and CEOs) and a number of human capital-, job- and firm-specific characteristics and performance variables for a sample of large UK firms listed on the London Stock Exchange. We assess the impact of the Cadbury proposals for greater disclosure of the details of executive pay schemes and the enhanced role of non-executive directors and remuneration committees to determine CEO pay. Early studies of CEO remuneration (e.g. Cosh, 1975) have tended to focus on linking remuneration solely to firm performance and size. Subsequent studies (e.g. Bartlett, Grant and Miller, 1992; Murphy, 1986, for the USA, and Main, 1991, for the UK) have found that both human capital- and firm-specific factors also impact on CEO remuneration, thereby implying that the earlier models may have suffered from an omitted variable problem (which may have exaggerated the size and significance of firm size and performance).

Following these more recent research findings, in our empirical assessment of the influence of the Cadbury recommendations on CEO pay we model explicitly for the effects of human capital-, job- and firm-specific characteristics and corporate governance variables, in addition to firm size and performance variables. Our analysis includes estimating separate CEO pay regression equations reflecting: (1) CEO pay levels; (2) changes in CEO pay levels; and (3) pay structure.

Our empirical analysis of the external market determinants of managerial pay begins with the assumption that shareholders demand paid managerial labour as a function of their total remuneration and their likely productivity. It is assumed that the latter is signalled by observable personal characteristics such as previous managerial experience, age, qualifications, track record and other human capital attributes which are difficult for low-quality agents to imitate. On the supply side, it is assumed that managers switch firms according to the characteristics of the firm and the salary and other emoluments offered. Important signals in this context will be observable characteristics such as past and anticipated firm growth/profits, size, job security, and expected career progression. If it is further assumed that the market for managers comprises a range of firms, each with managerial job opportunities and a range of potential managers, each with a range of human capital characteristics, then at equilibrium:

$$W = f(PC, JOB) \tag{2.1}$$

That is, the market-clearing level of remuneration (W) will be explained by the vectors of demand-relevant personal characteristics (PC) and supply-relevant job and firm characteristics (JOB).

In principle, an empirical estimation of equation (2.1) can be achieved by the following OLS regression:

$$\ln W_i = \alpha + \sum \beta_j PC_{ji} + \sum \beta_k JOB_{ki} + u_i \tag{2.2}$$

where $\ln W_i$ is the log of cash (salary or salary plus bonuses) remuneration for executive i, PC_{ji} the vector of personal and job history characteristics, JOB_{ki} the vector of job and firm characteristics, and u_i the error term.

The size and significance of the estimated coefficients will indicate those manager (PC) and/or employing firm (JOB) characteristics that have most influence upon market-wide remuneration levels. We estimate a remuneration equation along the lines of equation (2.2) for our sample of executives to obtain a proxy for the market rate of pay given the manager's personal and job/firm characteristics. A model such as that described by equation (2.2) does not explicitly include any performance or governance factors that may influence executive pay. Nevertheless, the equation can be augmented to include firm-specific performance ($Perf$) and governance characteristics (Gov) to determine whether these variables have a significant impact on the level of pay, i.e.

$$\ln W_i = \alpha + \sum \beta_j PC_{ji} + \sum \beta_k JOB_{ki} + \sum \beta_m Perf_{mi} + \sum \beta_n Gov_{ni} + u_i \tag{2.3}$$

The estimated pay levels obtained from equation (2.3) can then be utilised to examine the influence that external market comparisons and firm performance have upon the changes in pay levels over time.

If changes in pay are influenced by a combination of governance characteristics, changes in firm performance and adjustments towards the market rate then an equation of the following form will be appropriate:

$$\ln W_{it+1} - \ln W_{it} = \alpha + \sum \beta_j \Delta PC_{ji} + \sum \beta_k \Delta JOB_{ki} + \sum \beta_m \Delta Perf_{mi}$$

$$+ \sum \beta_n Gov_{ni} + \delta(\ln W_{it} - \ln W_{it}^*) + u_i \qquad (2.4)$$

where

ΔPC_{ji} = change in personnel/personal characteristics between t and $t + 1$
ΔJOB_{ki} = change in job/firm characteristics between t and $t + 1$
$\Delta Perf_{mi}$ = change in performance between t and $t + 1$
$(\ln W_{it} - \ln W_{it}^*)$ = the deviation of the executive's pay from the estimated market rate in the previous period
δ = the estimated adjustment factor by which pay moves towards the market rate in the subsequent period.

If remuneration committees attempt to move executive pay towards the market rate, then the coefficient on the deviation from the market wage in the previous period (δ) is expected to be significantly negative. Clearly, if there is full adjustment in a single period to the market rate, then $\delta = -1$ and if only partial adjustment δ will be between 0 and -1 (i.e. $0 > \delta > -1$).

This, however, makes the unrealistic assumption that the adjustment towards the market rate for both over- and underpaid executives is the same. As discussed earlier, the bidding-up hypothesis suggests otherwise. Namely, that there is likely to be an asymmetry in the adjustment process for those above and below the market rate and that those executives that have been paid above the market rate are unlikely to have their pay significantly reduced in subsequent periods. That is, δ for the overpaid executives (δ_o) will be greater than that of the underpaid executives (δ_u) and may in fact be greater than zero if they are in a position to maintain their relative pay advantage in future periods.

To test this hypothesis empirically, equation (2.4) can be adapted to separate out the under- and overpaid executives. This will facilitate the adjustment parameters for the under- and overpaid executives to be separately estimated in the following way:

$$\ln W_{it+1} - \ln W_{it} = \alpha + \sum \beta_j \Delta PC_{ji} + \sum \beta_k \Delta JOB_{ki} + \sum \beta_m \Delta Perf_{mi}$$

$$+ \sum \beta_n Gov_{ni} + \delta_u(\ln W_{it} - \ln W^*_{it})$$

$$+ \delta_o(\ln W_{it} - \ln W^*_{it}) + u_i \qquad (2.5)$$

where

$\delta_o(\ln W_{it} - \ln W^*_{it}) = $ all i's where $(\ln W_{it} - \ln W^*_{it}) > 0$, and 0 otherwise

$\delta_u(\ln W_{it} - \ln W^*_{it}) = $ all i's where $(\ln W_{it} - \ln W^*_{it}) < 0$, and 0 otherwise

However, because our proxy for the comparison rate of pay may be measured with error (i.e. is noisy) and, moreover, remuneration committees may only adjust executive pay in response to relatively large deviations (plus or minus) from the implied market rate of pay, a quadratic form may be a more appropriate test of the bidding-up hypothesis. Our empirical analysis, therefore, incorporates an alternative specification of equation (2.5) where the deviations from the implied external market comparison rates of pay, $(\ln W_{it} - \ln W^*_{it})$, are squared so that the estimated parameters δ_u and δ_o will measure the extent to which proportionately large deviations exhibit greater adjustments towards the market rate. As squaring the negative deviations relating to the underpaid executives removes the sign, to maintain comparability with the linear model, the squared deviations for these executives are then multiplied by minus 1.

For both the linear and quadratic specifications, empirical support for the bidding-up hypothesis would imply that:

$$\delta_u < 0 \text{ and } \delta_o > \delta_u$$

This implies further that for underpaid executives they have an overall positive pay adjustment as the product of a negative δ_u and a negative $(\ln W_{it} - \ln W^*_{it})$, and the reverse for overpaid executives.

Statistical evidence for the bidding-up hypothesis would be implied if, in addition to $\delta_u < 0$, it was also highly significant (i.e. a less than a 1% chance that the true relationship was $\delta_u = 0$), while the estimated parameter δ_o was either statistically indistinguishable from zero or, if overpaid executives are able to maintain their relative advantage in subsequent periods, $\delta_o > 0$.

The Sample

The basis of our sample of firms was all the listed companies in the *Times Top 1000* with December-January year ends that were in existence for the full two-year period from 1992 to 1993. Initially, these criteria produced a total sample of 223 companies. The sample was ultimately reduced to 199 companies with a complete and usable data set, representing 89% of the original sample. This small and unavoidable reduction in sample size was caused by a variety of reasons: (1) a few companies were not from the UK; (2) some companies had been merged with other companies since the publication of the *Times Top 1000*; (3) some companies did not have all the required variables for the period of study.

The requirement that each company in the sample should have a December-January year end was imposed to control for effects caused by heterogeneous year ends and to ensure that we could make use of the first-year post-Cadbury accounts to compare CEO remuneration models. It was also important that all companies in the sample were UK listed since (1) the Cadbury proposals were aimed at listed companies and (2) our empirical analysis makes use of shareholder returns data. The data sources included published annual accounts, the *Stock Exchange Year Book*, *The Hambro Corporate Register* and *Directors Guides* and *Data Stream*.

Broadly speaking, the variables collected can be grouped under the following categories:

1. Financial accounting
2. Market data
3. Ownership
4. CEO human capital
5. Firm-specific characteristics.

Descriptive statistics for the variables used in the empirical analysis are contained in Table 2.1. The sample companies have also been classified by industrial sector, using the two-digit SIC classification scheme. Over half the sample belongs to the general manufacturing sector, and over 30% are companies from the service sector. Finer industrial classification based on the SIC three-digit level has also been undertaken.

THE RESULTS

In this section we first present some initial descriptive statistics, followed by the main results and a discussion of their implications.

Descriptive Statistics

It is interesting to report on some of the main characteristics of our sample. In over 63% of the cases, financial institutions were the largest shareholders, and other forms of ownership (another plc, family/manage-

Table 2.1   Descriptive Statistics

Variable	mean	Std dev.	Min	Max
1993 Sales (£million)	175.8	440.2	55.5	4 766.0
1993 Capital Employed (£million)	162.8	238.0	1.8	975.0
1991 to 1993 Profit/Equity (%)	23.9	68.7	−54.0	693.0
No. of Directors	9.0	2.6	4.0	16.0
No. of Non-Executive Directors	3.9	1.7	0.0	10.0
1993 Salary Plus Bonus (£000s)	212.7	351.0	50.0	1 808.0
Age of Executive	54.7	6.9	40.0	81.0
Tenure	5.8	7.8	0.0	55.0
Type0 (non-chair executives)(%)	57.6	47.6	0.0	1.0
Type1 (Chair = CEO) (%)	15.6	36.4	0.0	1.0
Type2 (Executive Chair)(%)	26.8	44.4	0.0	1.0
1993 Shareholder Returns (%)	29.9	33.9	−84.7	170.2
% of Non-Executives in 1993	43.0	14.4	0.0	62.5
% of Executives on own Remuneration Committee	46.9	50.0	0.0	1.0

Number of observations = 224.

ment holdings, chairman or CEO major shareholder, and venture capital firm) account for the remainder. As can be seen from Table 2.2; the number of non-executive members of the board and the (reported) extent of compliance with the Cadbury code are positively related to size, as measured by sales in 1993.

Executive Company Positions

To examine further, though indirectly, the extent of influence that may be exerted by the company chairman, whether executive or non-executive, on various company decisions, we analysed the membership of the remuneration, audit and nomination committees, in addition to whether the chairman is also the chief executive officer. With respect to the latter, in 23% of the sample the chairman was the CEO, clearly casting some considerable doubt regarding the independence of the chairman and the effectiveness of monitoring CEOs in these companies. Interestingly, Table 2.2 (Pancl II) does not suggest that larger companies (in terms of sales) are any more likely to have a non-executive chairman than the smaller companies in the sample.

The position with respect to the membership of the above committees lends strong support to the doubts we have just expressed concerning independence and monitoring of UK executives. Our results indicate that in 41% of the cases the company chairman was also the chair of the

Table 2.2 Extent of Compliance and Type of Director by Size (1993 Sales)

PANEL I (Extent of compliance)

Sales quartile	Mean sales (£ms)	Full compliance	No compliance committee	States areas of non-compliance							Total non-compliers	Total
				No nominations committee	No advice for non-execs	No prof. directors' service contracts	Chairman is also CEO	Less than 3 non-execs serve on committees	Execs serve on audit committee	No non-compliers		
0.25	112.5	23	1	3	6	3	3	17	1	1	35	58
0.5	243.4	28	2	2	4	2	3	10	0	0	23	51
0.75	695.8	34	1	1	2	2	2	8	0	2	18	52
1	5141.9	37	0	0	3	2	4	4	0	0	13	50
Total		122	4	6	15	9	12	39	1	3	89	211

PANEL II (Type of director)

Sales quartile	Mean sales (£ms)	Number of firms with				Non-exec chairman	Chairman is CEO but not HPD	Chair is CEO and is HPD	Number of firms with		Total
		Less than 3 non-execs	3 non-execs	More than 3 non-execs	Total				Chair is not CEO nor HPD	Chair is not CEO but is HPD	
0.25	112.5	14	19	14	47	21	2	10	12	2	47
0.5	243.5	9	17	20	46	19	6	7	9	5	46
0.75	695.8	7	13	27	47	25	4	3	11	4	47
1	5141.9	4	5	38	47	12	3	8	18	6	47
Total		34	54	99	187	77	15	28	50	17	187

Note: some companies gave more than one area of non-compliance.

remuneration committee and in a further 33% he was a member of that committee. Similarly, the company chairman was the chair of the audit committee in 23% of the cases and a member of that committee in 29% of the cases. Finally, the company chairman was the chair of the nominations committee in 59% of the cases and a member of that committee in 24% of the cases. By virtue of chairing or being a member of such committees there is significant scope for senior UK company executives to exert considerable influence on the deliberations and decisions made in these committees, a concern that we elaborate on below. Yet another piece of evidence pointing to concern over the degree of independence of UK company executives can be gleaned from the extent to which companies are chaired by supposedly more neutral, or even watchful, non-executive directors. Our results show that only in 47% of the cases is the company chair a non-executive director, leaving the chairmanship of the remaining companies in the hands of executives. When this finding is linked to the earlier findings on committee membership the potential scope for executives to influence corporate decisions in ways that may be detrimental to shareholders' interests becomes even greater.

We also cross-tabulated the type of chairman (i.e. non-executive; executive and highest paid, etc.) by membership/chairmanship of the remuneration committee. When the chair was a non-executive director he was the chair of the committee in 61% of the cases and a member of that committee in 31% of the cases. When the chairman was an executive he chaired the remuneration committee in 27% of the cases and was a member of that committee in 35% of the cases (hence, potentially having some influence in over 60% of the cases). More detailed breakdown of that latter category (executive chairman) reveals some variations; thus, when the chairman was the same as the CEO, he chaired the committee in 17% of the cases and was a member of the committee in 35% of the cases, compared with 33% and 33% respectively when the executive chair was not the same as the CEO. While this might offer some limited comfort the point remains that executive chairmen are still in a position to wield considerable influence over the determination of their own pay as well as the salaries of other company managers.

Executive Pay

Table 2.3 presents some of the statistics on executive pay in our sample. The chairmen's salaries were examined for the years 1992 and 1993. As

Table 2.3 Non-executive and Executive Mean Salaries—1992 and 1993

Panel A

(Chairmen)	Non-executive chair	Chair is CEO but not HPD	Chair is CEO and HPD	Chair is not CEO nor HPD	Chair is not CEO but is HPD	Number of cases
Salary (1992)	£66.7K (77)	£192.69K (16)	£253.07K (29)	£174.11K (55)	£300.41K (17)	194
Salary (1993)	£63.03K (78)	£225.13K (16)	£278.31K (29)	£180.20K (55)	£306.41K (17)	195
Change in salary (1993-1992)	−£3.84K (77)	£32.44K (16)	£25.24K (29)	£6.09K (55)	£6.00K (17)	194

Panel B

(Executives)	CEO is HPD	CEO is Chair and HPD	CEO is not Chair but is HPD	CEO is not Chair but Chair is HPD[a]	Number of cases
Salary (1992)	£236.18K (142)	£253.07K (29)	£307.67K (15)	£238.00K (2)	188
Salary (1993)	£268.16K (146)	£278.31K (29)	£312.53K (15)	£240.00K (2)	192
Change in salary (1993-1992)	£32.74K (141)	£25.24K (29)	£4.87K (15)	£2.00K (2)	187

CEO = Chief Executive Officer.
HPD = highest paid director.
[a] Those are two cases where CEO salary was disclosed even though he was not the Chairman and the Chairman was the highest-paid director.

expected, the mean of the salaries for non-executive chairmen was considerably lower than that of executive chairmen. As we are primarily concerned with executive pay, these non-executive chairmen are excluded from our empirical analysis of the levels and changes in executive pay reported later. It is worth noting that there are variations in the salary means for different types of executive chairmen. In both years, the highest average salaries were awarded to the chairmen who, though not the CEOs, were nevertheless identified as also being the highest-paid directors of their companies, followed by the chairs who were both the CEOs and the highest-paid directors, then the chairs who were the CEOs but not the highest-paid directors, and finally, the lowest paid were those chairs who were neither CEOs nor the highest-paid directors.

It is also worth noting the changes (first differences) in the chair salaries in 1993 compared to 1992. For the non-executive chairmen, their average salaries *went down* by £3.84K. While for some individuals, particularly chairmen that ceased being executives during the previous year, their pay will have fallen, few other individuals in the sample actually experienced a fall in pay. These results largely reflect the simple fact that, as recommended by the Cadbury Report, a number of companies in the sample appointed non-executive chairmen for the first time during the year. Considering the various types of executive chairmen, those who got the highest increase were the chairs who were also the CEOs but not the highest-paid directors (£32.4K), followed by the chairs who were *not* CEOs but were the highest-paid directors (£25.2K), with the remaining two categories (chair not the same as CEO whether or not highest-paid director) getting by far the smallest increase (£6K). This suggests, at least at this stage of the analysis, that assuming the CEO responsibilities by the chairmen provides the highest financial rewards.

The Multivariate Results

The empirical estimation of the models described in equations (2.3) to (2.5) have been based on data relating to 224 of the total of 284 *executive* directors detailed earlier. Clearly, the range of available explanatory variables that could be used to capture the different dimensions of firm performance, governance and executive's human capital is extensive. Though alternative empirical specifications of the models presented in this chapter have been undertaken, we have chosen not to report them since (1) they did not result in materially different results and/or (2) the theoretical rationale for their inclusion and the expected relationship to the dependent variables was ambiguous. The empirical results relating to the levels of pay in 1992 and 1993 are presented in Table 2.4 for respectively (Panel I) total cash remuneration (salary plus bonus) and (Panel II) salary only. The results for the changes in pay equations are presented in Table 2.5 for respectively (Panel I) total pay and (Panel II) salary only.

Executive Pay Levels in 1992 and 1993

The empirical results for the pay level estimates shown in Table 2.4 indicate that in both 1992 and 1993, approximately 56% of the cross-sectional variance in the levels of executive pay can be explained by an equation containing the following nine variables:

- Log of Sales (a measure of firm size and easily the most important factor driving the level of pay)
- Log of Capital Employed (an alternative measure of firm size which, though highly correlated with Sales, is nevertheless, highly significant)
- Average (over 3 years) return on equity (not significant in any equation)
- Log shareholder returns (significant in 1992 but not 1993)
- Executive's age (though not significant, the estimated parameters indicate that the relationship is of an inverted U-shape with pay at a maximum for executives 46 to 47 years old)
- Job type (relative to the reference category, CEOs who are not also chairmen, the significantly positive coefficients on the two dummy variables, type2 and type1 representing respectively executive chairmen and chairmen that are also the CEO, indicates that individuals occupying these latter two positions have significantly higher pay than the non-chairman CEOs)
- Short tenure (a dummy variable indicating which individuals had been in post for only one year or less in 1992)
- The proportion of non-executive members of the board
- Whether the executive was a member of the remuneration committee.

The size of the coefficients on each of these variables were statistically similar in both 1992 and 1993, whether or not the dependent variable was total cash remuneration (salary plus bonus) or simply salary excluding bonus. This, along with the fact that the cross-sectional estimates were able to explain a high proportion of the variance in the pay levels of executives and that size rather than firm performance variables were of most significance, suggests that executive pay levels involve a large element of external market comparison with the pay of other executives in similar-sized firms.

Table 2.4 Estimation of Executive Pay Levels 1992 and 1993

Variable	1992		1993	
	Coefficient	t-value	Coefficient	t-value
Panel I				
Dependent variable = ln W where W = salary plus bonus ($N = 224$)				
Constant	−0.969	0.85	−1.527	0.98
ln (Sales)	0.231	6.17***	0.203	5.34***
ln (Capital Employed)	0.119	3.59***	0.138	3.27***
Profit/Equity (%)	0.005	0.12	0.009	0.20
ln (Returns)	0.280	3.38***	0.151	1.62*
Age	0.036	0.78	0.052	0.91
Age2	−0.391E-3	0.95	−0.473E-3	0.91
Type1 (Chair = CEO)	0.902	3.68***	0.971	3.27***
Type2 (Executive chairman)	0.506	2.23**	0.495	1.74*
Tenure < =1	−0.161	1.59	−0.110	1.64*
Prop of Non-Execs	0.627	2.85***	0.452	2.28**
Rem Committee Member	−0.105	1.63*	−0.116	2.00**
$\bar{R}^2 =$	56.5		56.4	
F-ratio (with 11 and 212 d.o.f.) =	27.3		27.3	
Panel II				
Dependent variable = ln W where W = salary only ($N = 224$)				
Constant	−0.534	0.45	−1.189	0.87
ln (Sales)	0.236	5.59***	0.198	5.66***
ln (Capital Employed)	0.117	3.56***	0.149	4.02***
Profit/Equity (%)	0.017	0.42	0.016	0.42
ln (Returns)	0.177	2.05**	0.032	0.40
Age	0.013	0.27	0.035	0.69
Age2	−0.219E-3	0.49	−0.352E-3	0.76
Type1 (Chair = CEO)	0.900	3.82***	1.092	4.19***
Type2 (Executive chairman)	0.538	2.50**	0.696	2.77***
Tenure < =1	−0.191	1.53	−0.086	1.41
Prop of Non-Execs	0.898	3.78***	0.528	3.14***
Rem Committee Member	−0.060	1.01	−0.123	2.48**
$\bar{R}^2 =$	52.9		62.7	
F-ratio (with 11 and 212 d.o.f.) =	23.8		35.0	

Note: t-values based on White's (1980) adjustment for heteroskedasticity.

Changes in Executive Pay 1992 to 1993

In order to test the relative explanatory power of the (1) pay-for-performance and (2) market comparison and 'bidding-up' hypotheses, a proxy for the market comparison level of pay is required. This is achieved by utilising the deviation from the implied 'market rate' of pay in 1992 (i.e. the residuals from the 1992 pay-level equations) shown in Table 2.4. If the estimated pay-level equation for 1992 is a reasonable approximation to the market rate, then these residuals will indicate those executives that appeared to be under- or over-paid relative to the market. Note that the high explanatory power of the 1992 pay-levels model (which is able to explain approximately 56% of the cross-sectional variance in pay) suggests that the residuals will be a reasonable proxy for our purposes.

If market comparisons are the main drivers of executive pay, then these residuals will be negatively related to changes in pay in 1993. This, of course, assumes that the adjustment towards the market rate is identical for both under- and over-paid executives. Model 1 in Table 2.4 incorporates this hypothesis. However, according to the bidding-up hypothesis, an asymmetry in adjustments towards the market rate of pay can be expected between the under- and over-paid executives. Models 2 and 3 in Table 2.5 incorporate, respectively, the linear and quadratic specifications for testing the bidding-up hypothesis which, it will be recalled, suggests that only the adjustment factor for the relatively underpaid executives will be significantly negative.

As can be seen from Table 2.5, the changes in pay estimates indicate strong support for:

- The bidding-up hypothesis (in that relatively underpaid executives in 1992 experience an additional increase in pay in 1993 which is approximately 50% of the previous year's deviation from the estimated market rate). This result is robust to changes in the previous-period comparison of the pay-level estimation model and in the number of other explanatory variables included in the changes in the pay model. The greatly increased statistical significance of the quadratic specification of the bidding-up hypothesis indicates that high underpayments relative to the market in 1992 are associated with a more than proportionate movement towards the market rate in 1993.
- The remuneration committee appears to be tying some element of the change in pay (both salary and salary plus bonus) to shareholder returns, though, as might be expected, the relationship is much stronger when bonuses are included in the pay variable.
- Firms with a higher proportion of non-executive members on the board

award relatively smaller increases in pay after controlling for changes in sales growth, shareholder returns and the 'bidding-up' phenomenon.

An important function of independent non-executives and one of the main reasons for setting up remuneration committees was to make a significant element of executive pay more dependent upon firm performance. Additional analyses relating to whether various governance factors were associated with a stronger relationship between changes in pay and firm performance were undertaken. Interaction terms consisting of various firm performance measures (sales growth, profits and shareholder returns) and governance variables were added to the models. However, none of the coefficients on these interaction terms were statistically significant, which suggests that the modest relationship detailed above between changes in pay and firm performance (shareholder returns) was not altered by the existence of these governance factors.

CONCLUSIONS

This chapter has examined the relationship between executive remuneration and corporate and human capital characteristics in a large sample of UK companies following the implementation of the Cadbury committees recommendations. The main results indicate that:

1. The levels of executive pay are largely driven by firm size variables (the proportion of non-executives being positively correlated with firm size).
2. The high explanatory power and similarity of the 1992 and 1993 executive pay-level equations suggest that external market executive pay comparisons are of far greater importance in explaining pay levels than firm performance variables.
3. The importance of external market pay comparisons is supported when changes in pay are examined. The results indicate strong support for the 'bidding-up' hypothesis, particularly with respect to changes in pay excluding bonuses, in relation to pay adjustments for those executives that appeared to be underpaid in the previous period.
4. Firm performance (shareholder returns) is, however, also of importance in explaining changes in executive pay, particularly in relation to our pay measure that includes the cash bonus element.
5. The characteristics of the remuneration committee and other governance variables, either alone or when included as interaction terms with firm performance variables, do not result in a stronger relationship between changes in pay and firm performance.

Table 2.5 Estimation of Executive Pay Changes 1992 to 1993

Variable	Model 1		Model 2		Model 3	
	Coefficient	t-value	Coefficient	t-value	Coefficient	t-value
Panel 1 Dep Var = Salary plus Bonus ($n = 224$)						
Constant	0.004	0.02	0.072	1.45	0.006	0.36
Change in ln (Sales)	0.129	0.83	0.091	0.66	0.041	0.31
Change in Profit/Equity (%)	−0.009	0.45	−0.011	0.49	−0.011	0.52
ln (Returns)	0.260	4.82***	0.270	5.04***	0.244	4.73***
Short Tenure $<=1$ year in 1992	0.135	2.56***	0.111	2.70***	0.077	1.95*
Change in Personnel 1992 to 1993	−0.345	2.52**	−0.316	2.27**	−0.329	2.33**
Change in Job Specification	−0.199	2.01**	−0.222	2.18***	−0.218	2.55**
(ln W_{92} − ln W^*_{92})	−0.278	2.62***				
(ln W_{92} − ln W^*_{92}) > 0			−0.013	0.13	−0.129	1.53
(ln W_{92} − ln W^*_{92}) < 0			−0.498	2.74***	−0.323	22.29**
$\bar{R}^2$ =	27.8		32.4		42.1	
F-ratio =	13.2		14.4		21.4	

Panel II: Salary only

Constant	−0.000	0.01	−0.121	3.05***	0.016	1.00
Change in ln (Sales)	0.150	1.16	0.093	0.91	0.018	0.19
Change in Profit/Equity (%)	−0.006	0.33	−0.008	0.46	−0.009	0.45
ln (Returns)	0.102	2.21**	0.124	2.90***	0.085	2.10**
Short Tenure $<=1$ year in 1992	0.158	2.78***	0.112	2.78***	0.081	1.93*
Change in Personnel 1992 to 1993			−0.256	2.02**	−0.300	2.32**
Change in Job Specification	−0.280	2.25**	−0.123	1.38	−0.132	2.04**
$(\ln W_{92} - \ln W^*_{92})$	−0.102	1.00				
$(\ln W_{92} - \ln W^*_{92}) > 0$	−0.455	2.86***	0.071	0.82	−0.180	2.43**
$(\ln W_{92} - \ln W^*_{92}) < 0$			−0.736	4.89***	−0.241	34.66**
$R^2 =$	27.8		57.0		64.6	
F-ratio $=$	13.2		37.9		51.9	

Note
* —significant at the 90% level
** —significant at the 95% level
*** —significant at the 98% level

Our results clearly suggest that the 'bidding-up' phenonenon is robust. It is important to reiterate that the bidding-up process does not necessarily imply that non-executive directors serving on the remuneration committees of UK companies lack independence. A significant element of bidding up is probably inevitable given the widespread use by remuneration committees of outside consultants. The recommendations of outside pay consultants can only be based upon comparisons with the remuneration levels of comparable individuals employed by firms that appear to be 'similar' to an outsider. In this regard, 'similar' appears to mean primarily 'similar-sized firms'. On the basis of these fairly blunt external market comparisons, it is perhaps not surprising that apparently overpaid individuals do not suffer a significant reduction in the subsequent period's pay award. Simply from a motivational standpoint, the possible costs are likely to be perceived to be greater than any benefits that might accrue to the firm's shareholders from reducing the pay of senior executives.

A major limitation of our analysis is that we have not attempted to incorporate the non-cash elements (e.g. options or deferred bonuses) of the senior executive's total remuneration package. Since the value of an executive's share options will necessarily vary quite closely with changes in the market value of the company's shares, this will create a much greater degree of alignment between executive wealth and shareholder value. Hence, the relatively modest relationship found to exist in this study between pay and firm performance may be considerably strengthened by the inclusion of share option awards.

NOTES

1. A number of other theoretical perspectives suggest, however, that executive pay will not be closely linked to firm performance measures. For example, Marginal Productivity, Efficiency Wage, Tournament, Figurehead and Signalling theories all predict that executive salaries will be largely driven by factors other than firm performance (see Gomez-Mejia, 1994, for a review).
2. With the exception of Tournament theory, which has a predominantly internal labour market focus, all the theoretical frameworks mentioned in note 1 suggest that the 'going rate' determined by the external managerial labour market will have an important influence in the setting of executive pay.
3. Due to problems of data availability and difficult-to-resolve valuation issues relating to executive share option awards, none of these studies have attempted to construct and empirically test a comprehensive measure of the change in executive wealth arising from his or her employment. The sole

exception, a (forthcoming) paper by Main *et al.* (1996), does in fact report an extremely strong link between an executive's change in wealth (total cash remuneration plus the change in the value of shares and executive share option holdings) and changes in shareholder wealth.

4. Several US studies have reported results consistent with the hypotheses that takeovers and outside (i.e. non-executive) directors (Martin and McConnell, 1991; Weisbach, 1988; Kini, Kracaw and Mian, 1995) and ownership structures (Demsetz and Lehn, 1985; Shivdasani, 1993) appear to serve as substitute control mechanisms.

5. Formal debtholder intervention is normally only possible after a contractual breach has occurred, such as the violation of an accounting-based covenant. Given the high degree of 'flexibility' associated with financial reporting standards, executives have significant scope to delay reporting (or even to avoid altogether) formal breaches which would lead to debtholder intervention.

6. For a review of the conflicting functions expected to non-executive directors under UK company law, see Ezzamel and Watson (1996).

REFERENCES

Antle, R. and Smith, A. (1986) An empirical investigation of the relative performance evaluation of corporate executives. *Journal of Accounting Research*, **24**, 1–39.

Bankar, R. and Datar, S. (1989) Sensitivity, precision and linear aggregation of signals for performance evaluation. *Journal of Accounting Research*, **27**, 21–39.

Barro, J.R. and Barro, R.J. (1990) Pay, performance and turnover of bank CEOs. *Journal of Labour Economics*, **8**, October, 448–81.

Bartlett, R., Grant, J. and Miller, T. (1992) The earnings of top executives: compensating differentials for risky business. *Quarterly Review of Economics and Finance*, **32**, 38–49.

Baumol, W.J.L. (1967) *Business Behavior, Value and Growth*, revised version, New York: Macmillan.

Benson, G. (1985) The self-serving management hypothesis. *Journal of Accounting and Economics*, **7**, 67–84.

Berle, A. and Means, G. (1932) *The Modern Corporation and Private Property*, New York: Macmillan.

Byrd, J.W. and Hickman, K.A. (1992) Do outside directors monitor managers? *Journal of Financial Economics*, **32**, 195–221.

Cadbury Committee (1992) *Report on the Committee on the Financial Aspects of Corporate Governance*, Draft Report, May, Final Report, December, London: Gee and Co.

Ciscel, D.H. and Carroll, T.M. (1980) The determinants of executive salaries: an econometric survey. *Review of Economics and Statistics*, February, 7–13.

Charkham, J. (1989) Corporate governance and the market for control of companies. Bank of England Panel Paper 25, March.

Clinch, G. (1991) Employee compensation and firms' research and development activity. *Journal of Accounting Research*, **27**, 59–78.

Conyon, M. and Leech, D. (1994) Top pay, company performance and corporate governance. *Oxford Bulletin of Economics and Statistics*, **56**, 229–47.

Cosh, A. (1975) The remuneration of chief executives in the United Kingdom. *Economic Journal*, **85**, No. 1, 75–94.

Cosh, A. and Hughes, A. (1987) The anatomy of corporate control: directors, shareholders and executive remuneration of giant US and UK corporations. *Cambridge Journal of Economics*, **11**, 285–313.

Coughlan, A. and Schmidt, R. (1985) Executive compensation, management turnover and performance. *Journal of Accounting and Economics*, **7**, 43–66.

Davis, E. and Kay, J. (1993) Corporate governance, take-overs, and the role of the non-executive director. In Bishop and Kay, J. (eds), *European Mergers and Merger Policy*, Oxford: Oxford University Press.

Demsetz, H. and Lehn, K. (1985) The structure of corporate ownership: causes and consequences. *Journal of Political Economy*, **93**, 1155–77.

Ezzamel, M. and Watson, R. (1996) Wearing two hats: the conflicting management and control roles of non-executive directors. Chapter 5 in Keasey, K., Thompson, S. and Wright, M. (eds), *Corporate Governance*, Oxford: Oxford University Press.

Fama, E.F. (1980) Agency problems and the theory of the firm. *Journal of Political Economy*, 280–307.

Fama, E.F. and Jensen, M.C. (1983a) Separation of ownership and control. *Journal of Law and Economics*, **26**, 301–26.

Fama, E.F. and Jensen, M.C. (1983b) Agency problems and residual claims. *Journal of Law and Economics*, **26**, 327–52.

Forbes, W. and Watson, R. (1993) Managerial remuneration and corporate governance: a review of the issues, evidence and Cadbury Committee proposals. *Accounting and Business Research*, **23**, 331–8.

Gomez-Mejia, L. (1994) Executive compensation: a reassessment and a future research agenda. *Research in Personnel and Human Resources Management*, **12**, 331–8.

Gregg, P., Machin, S. and Szymanski, S. (1993) The disappearing relationship between directors' pay and corporate performance. *British Journal of Industrial Relations*, **31**, 1–9.

Grossman, S. and Hart, O. (1982) Takeover bids, the free-rider problem, and the theory of the corporation. *Bell Journal of Economics*, **11**, 42–64.

Hirshleiffer, D. and Suh, Y. (1992) Risk, managerial effort, and project choice. *Journal of Financial Intermediation*, **2**, 308–45.

Holmstrom, B. (1979) Moral hazard and observability. *Bell Journal of Economics*, **10**, Spring, 74–91.

Incomes Data Services (IDS) (1993), *Setting Pay at the Top*.

Jensen, M.C. (1986) Agency costs of free cash flow, corporate finance and takeovers. *American Economic Review*, **76**, May, 323–9.

Jensen, M.C. (1989) The eclipse of the public corporation. *Harvard Business Review*, October, 61–74.

Jensen, M.C. and Meckling, W. (1976) The theory of the firm: managerial behaviour, agency costs and ownership structure. *Journal of Financial Economics*, 3, 305–60.

Jensen, M.C. and Murphy, K.J. (1990) Performance pay and top management incentives. *Journal of Political Economy*, **98**, No. 2, 225–64.

Kini, O., Kracaw, W. and Mian, S. (1995) Corporate takeovers, firm performance and board composition. *Journal of Corporate Finance*, **1**, 383–412.

Lewellen, W.G. and Huntsman, B. (1970) Managerial pay and corporate performance. *American Economic Review*, **60**, 710–20.

Main, B.G.M. (1991) Top executive pay and performance. *Managerial and Decision Economics*, **12**, 219–29.

Main, B.G.M., Bruce, A. and Buck, T. (1996) Total board remuneration and company performance. *Economic Journal*, forthcoming.

Main, B.G.M. and Johnston, J. (1991) Remuneration committees and corporate governance. University of Edinburgh Discussion Paper, December.

Main, B.G.M. and Johnston, J. (1992) The remuneration committee as an instrument of corporate governance. David Hume Institute, University of Edinburgh, Occasional Paper.

Main, B.G.M. and Johnston, J. (1993) Remuneration committees and corporate governance. *Accounting and Business Research*, **23**, No. 91A, 351–62.

Martin, K. and McConnell, J. (1991) Corporate performance, takeovers and management turnover. *Journal of Finance*, **46**, 671–87.

Masson, R.T. (1971) Executive motivations, earnings and consequent equity performance. *Journal of Political Economy*, **79**, 1278–92.

Morck, R., Shleifer, A. and Vishney, R.W. (1989) Alternative mechanisms for corporate control. *American Economic Review*, **79**, 842–52.

Mueller, D. (1979) *Public Choice*, New York: Cambridge University Press.

Murphy, K.J. (1985) Corporate performance and managerial remuneration: an empirical analysis. *Journal of Accounting and Economics*, **7**, 11–42.

Murphy, K.J. (1986) Incentives, learning and compensation: a theoretical and empirical investigation of managerial labor markets. *Bell Journal of Economics*, **17**, 59–76.

Ogden, S. and Watson, R. (1996) The relationship between changes in incentive structures, executive pay and corporate performance: some evidence from the privatised water industry in England and Wales. *Journal of Business Finance and Accounting*. **23**, 721–51.

O'Reilley, C., Main, B. and Crystal, G. (1988) CEO salaries as tournaments and social comparisons: a tale of two theories. *Administrative Science Quarterly*, **33**, 257–74.

Pavlik, E.L., Scott, T. and Tiessen, P. (1993) Executive compensation: issues and research. *Journal of Accounting Literature*, **12**, 131–89.

Shivdasani, A. (1993) Board composition, ownership structure and hostile takeovers. *Journal of Accounting and Economics*, **16**, 167–208.

Stiglitz, J.E. (1985) Credit markets and the control of capital. *Journal of Money, Credit and Banking*, **17**, 133–52.

Tatton, A. (1992) Top people's pay is called to account. *Independent on Sunday*, 20 September 1992, p. 21.

Thompson, S. and Wright, M. (1995) Corporate governance: the role of restructuring transactions. *Economic Journal*, **105**, 690–703.

Weisbach, M. (1988) Outside directors and CEO turnover. *Journal of Financial Economics*, **20**, 431–60.

White H. (1980) A heteroskedasticity-consistent covariance matrix estimator and a direct test for heteroskedasticity. *Econometrica*, **48**, 817–38.

Wruck, K. (1990) Financial distress, reorganisation and organizational efficiency. *Journal of Financial Economics*, **27**, 419–44.

3

Audit Committees in Smaller Listed Companies

PAUL COLLIER

INTRODUCTION

The Cadbury Committee (1992) not only laid considerable stress on audit committees and their role in improving financial reporting and corporate governance but also recommended that all listed companies should establish an effective audit committee. The Cadbury recommendations were given additional weight when the Stock Exchange featured the Code of Best Practice in its continuing obligations for listed companies (paragraph 12.43j of the new listing rules). However, compliance is not mandatory and the only mandatory requirement is for the company to state its degree of compliance so that users of the accounts are aware of the situation. The involvement of the Stock Exchange is limited to ensuring that the degree of compliance is stated and that reasons are given for any non-compliance. The Stock Exchange does not specify the standard of the corporate governance systems employed, nor does it determine the adequacy of any reasons given for non-compliance. Action is only taken against companies that fail to report fully in accordance with paragraph 12.43(j).

Several commentators (see, for example, the points raised by both the Association of Chartered Certified Accountants (ACCA) and the City

Corporate Governance: Responsibilities, Risks and Remuneration. Edited by Kevin Keasey and Mike Wright © 1997 John Wiley & Sons Ltd.

Group for Small Companies (CISCO) (*Accountancy Age*, 1993)) have suggested that the Cadbury recommendations, including the audit committee requirement, are designed for larger quoted companies and may well prove too costly or impractical for smaller companies. The CISCO code (CISCO, 1993) modified some elements of the Cadbury Code to make them more relevant to smaller listed companies which were defined as those outside the FTSE 350 index. CISCO acknowledges that for many companies at the upper end of the size limit there should be no difficulties in complying with the Code but for companies at the lower end of the scale there may well be problems.

CISCO broadly agreed with Cadbury about audit committees and acknowledged that 'it is fundamental that an audit committee is established and that all non-executive directors are members of it'. However, CISCO modified the Code by suggesting that the membership need not be restricted to non-executive directors provided that a non-executive director is appointed as chairman of the audit committee, and that as part of the arrangements, non-executive directors have meetings with the company's auditors at which executive directors are not present. Further, where a company has a small board (that is, less than five members) the audit committee may also assume the duties of the remuneration committee and nomination committee.

The issues explored in this chapter relate to the impact of the audit committee requirements of the Cadbury recommendations on smaller listed companies. In particular, the chapter analyses a number of case studies to provide detailed information on (1) the structure of small company boards; (2) the organisation and operation of audit committees in small companies; and (3) an insight into the opinions of a limited number of small-company finance directors and non-executive directors.

SUMMARY OF EXISTING THEORY AND EMPIRICAL EVIDENCE

The impact of the recommendations that smaller listed companies should improve corporate governance by the formation of audit committees has been discussed by policy makers. For example, the Treadway Commission (1987, p. 29) observed that imposing corporate governance regulations on companies gave the long-term benefits of enhanced corporate control and ethical business conduct. The imposition of the costs of implementing its recommendations on businesses was justified by noting that while implementation costs can be quantified, the costs of non-implementation in terms of a loss of investor confidence in corporate management and the financial reporting system cannot. However, as this confidence is fundamental to the operation of the capital markets on which companies rely, it is certain that the costs outweigh the benefits. Treadway (1987, p. 29) also anticipated that smaller companies might bear a disproportionate share of the costs of implementing its recommendations and judged that this was reasonable as smaller companies may have a disproportionately greater risk of fraudulent financial reporting and thus reap proportionately greater benefits. The recommendations will help smaller companies run in a more orderly fashion and thereby improve their access to capital markets. In contrast, the Cadbury Committee provided no discussion of the costs of their recommendations.

The academic literature on audit committees also acknowledges the problem. The theoretical arguments against audit committees were summarised by Bradbury (1990), who pointed out that the requirement for companies to operate an audit committee can (1) impose costs unevenly across companies if differences exist between companies in the costs and benefits of monitoring packages; (2) lead to companies transferring resources from existing, and perhaps more effective, monitoring activities on the assumption that monitoring expenditure is limited; and (3) prevent companies from signalling information by the choice of an audit committee as a monitoring mechanism. Further, both Pincus, Rubarsky and Wong (1989) and Collier (1993) noted that although major companies may not find the burden imposed by the Cadbury requirement for an audit committee material, the costs of forming an audit committee among smaller listed companies may well act as a disincentive to being listed and explain why surveys of the *Times Top 1000* (e.g. Marrian, 1988; Bank of England, 1988) have shown that only a small minority of companies outside the *Times Top 250* have an audit committee. Beyond this little is known about audit committees in smaller listed companies and it is this knowledge gap that this chapter seeks to rectify.

THE RESEARCH METHODS

The research has two stages: (1) a questionnaire to see if there are differences between the boards and audit committees of larger and smaller listed companies; and (2) an examination through case studies of the operation of audit committees in smaller listed companies. The population for the first-stage circularisation was based on the 1653 listed companies from Table 3.1 which was derived from the then current *Quality of Markets Companies Book* (The International Stock Exchange of the United Kingdom and the Republic of Ireland Limited, 1993).

The population was reduced to 1089 through the exclusion of the Financial Group, Investment Trusts, and Irish equities. The cut-off between larger and smaller listed companies was set at a market value of £100 million. At this level around two thirds of the companies by number but only 4.3% by value are defined as smaller listed companies. Such companies are important in terms of numbers if not of market value.

The case study methodology was chosen for investigating audit committees in smaller listed companies as the merits of the approach have been well established by a number of authors (e.g. Mohr, 1985; Kaplan, 1984, 1986; Rickwood, Coates and Stacey, 1987; Holland, 1993). However, when reviewing the results it must be remembered that the cases are not necessarily representative due, for example, to the failure to gain access to all the selected cases and the small proportion of the population covered. The smaller listed companies approached for co-operation with the case study research were chosen from the smaller listed companies randomly selected in the first stage. Twenty companies were selected intuitively with the objective of providing a mix of companies with respect to their market value, and the age of their audit committee. A letter requesting assistance was sent to each company. Companies who responded positively were subsequently sent a protocol which indicated the areas to be covered in the interview.

Table 3.1 Distribution of Companies by Market Value at 30 June 1993

Market value (£m)	No. of companies	%	Equity market value (£m)	%	% of total turnover
Over 2000	72	4.4	424 381	62.2	63.0
500–2000	150	9.0	152 699	22.4	26.5
100–500	342	20.8	75 626	11.1	7.7
50–100	202	12.2	14 524	2.1	1.3
Less than 50	887	53.6	15 325	2.2	1.5
Total	1653	100.0	682 555	100.0	100.0

Adapted from Table C in *Quality of Markets Companies Book* (1993, p. 19).

THE SURVEY RESULTS

The results of the survey showed that 85% of larger listed companies and 83% of smaller listed companies had formed an audit committee by May 1994. Although the proportion of companies with an audit committee are broadly similar as between larger and smaller listed companies, Table 3.2 shows that smaller listed companies rarely sought to form audit committees prior to the pressure exerted by Cadbury. Indeed, over 60% of the smaller companies which formed an audit committee between 1991 and 1993 did so in 1993 after the recommendation that all listed companies should form audit committees had been issued.

Table 3.3, which is based on information obtained from the annual report and accounts of the companies, shows that there are also clear differences in the membership of both the board and the audit committee[1]. These findings suggest that the procedures and practices of the audit committee in smaller listed companies differ from those described in Collier (1993).

Table 3.2 The Timing of Audit Committee Formation

Period of formation	% of larger listed companies	% of smaller listed companies
Pre-1980	7	–
1980 to 1990	50	16
1991 to 1993	43	84
	100	100

Table 3.3 Information on Board Structures

Number of	Mean for larger listed companies	Mean for smaller listed companies
Executive directors	5.82	4.31
Non-executive directors	3.79	2.84
Executives and non-executives	9.61	7.15
Members of the audit committee	3.92	3.16

THE PROFILE OF THE CASE STUDY COMPANIES

Of the twenty smaller listed companies which were approached eight agreed to participate in the project. Table 3.4 shows the case studies provide a spread with respect to audit committee age and market value. The oldest audit committee had been formed in the 1980s but others were set up in or after 1990 with three being constituted after the Cadbury report. All the companies had significant numbers of shareholders. However, in many cases the concentration of shareholders was even greater than that indicated by the substantial shareholders figures. For example, at C, E and F over 75%, 80% and 90% of shares respectively were held by institutions. The extent to which directors had substantial ownership interests also varied. For example, no directors at C or D had significant holdings of the companies' shares; whereas at E, F, G and H, one or more directors had interests in excess of the 3% limit for substantial holdings, and at A and B there are one or more directors with large shareholdings which do not exceed the 3% limit. The majority of the companies (5/8) had a 'Big-Six' firm as their group auditor. There was general agreement among these companies that 'Big-Six' firms had greater expertise across a range of services and a better reputation. More specifically, A and E stated that an international audit firm was essential for the proper servicing of the group on a worldwide basis. However, G which employed a 'Big-Six' firm for the group audit used local auditors in its overseas subsidiaries. The use of local firms for overseas subsidiaries was not confined to G and 'Big-Six' firms as B and F, which had non 'Big-Six' group auditors, both used local auditors overseas. None of the companies selected had an

Table 3.4

Ref.	Year of formation	Market value (£m)	Approx no. of share-holders	Approx % held by substantial shareholders	Approx no. of employees	Spread of group ops
A	1991	10–20	2000	40	Under 50	Intnl
B	Pre-1985	50–100	1000	60	1000	Intnl
C	1992	50–100	1000	45	1000	UK
D	1992	20–50	1000	60	700	UK
E	N/A	20–50	2000	15	400	Intnl
F	N/A	Below 10	1500	45	200	Intnl
G	1990	10–20	3000	30	400	Intnl
H	1993	Below 10	1500	35	300	UK

internal auditor or internal audit department, although some admitted to giving the matter serious consideration.

THE BOARDS OF THE CASE STUDY COMPANIES

Surveys by the Bank of England (see, for example, the Bank of England, 1988) show that the number of non-executive directors on boards is growing but that there is little consistency in the structure of UK large company boards. Table 3.5 shows that the boards of the smaller listed companies covered by the research fell into two groups. The two largest companies, based on market value (B and C), had large boards of 12 and 10 members, respectively, whereas the remainder had boards of between four and seven members. The Institute of Chartered Accountants in England and Wales (ICAEW, 1991) study group on the changing role of the non-executive director recommended that non-executive directors should comprise around a third of the board and ideally there should be at least three non-executive directors. The first part of this target was met by all the companies, but only three of the eight companies interviewed met the second part. However, all companies met the CISCO (1993, p. 6) guidance which recommends that smaller companies should have at least two non-executive directors and probably conformed with the Cadbury code which merely states that 'The board should include non-executive directors of sufficient calibre and number for their views to carry significant weight in the board's decisions'.

The companies were generally satisfied with the size and composition of their board, although three companies were considering the possibility of an additional non-executive director. The search for an additional non-executive director was usually motivated by business reasons such as the need to increase contacts and customers rather than a response to Cadbury. A consistent theme among the smaller companies was that non-executive directors must add value to the company rather than be an

Table 3.5 Board Size at the Case Study Companies

	Company							
	A	B	C	D	E	F	G	H
Executive directors	3	6	3	2	3	2	3	4
Non-executive directors	2	6	7	2	2	2	2	3
Total board	5	12	10	4	5	4	5	7

overhead—a requirement which restricted the pool of suitable candidates. A further problem in the companies related to the Cadbury recommendation that the majority of non-executive directors should be 'independent' of management and free of any relationship that might materially interfere with the exercise of their independent judgement. Some of the non-executives had strong historical ties with the company, others represented a significant shareholder (usually an institutional investor) and a number were in related businesses.

The Code of Best Practice issued by Cadbury suggested 'There should be a clearly accepted division of responsibilities at the head of a company, which will ensure a balance of power and authority, such that no one individual has unfettered powers of decision. Where the chairman is also chief executive, it is essential that there should be a strong and independent element on the board, with a recognised senior member' (s. 1.2, p. 58). The role of chairman and managing director was combined in half the companies. The situation reflects the small size of the companies and the need for strict cost control. The interviewees admitted to being aware of the dangers involved in this concentration of power. In three out of the four cases the position was under review and one company split the post after the interview. The existence of a director who combined the role of chairman and chief executive did not appear to influence audit committee practice or whether the auditor was a 'Big-Six' auditor. In the former case, three of the four companies with a chairman/chief executive had a separate audit committee, and in the latter case, two of the four companies with a chairman/chief executive had a 'Big-Six' auditor.

The Cadbury recommendations had influenced board structures with all the companies having a remuneration committee and three quarters a separate audit committee. The membership of these committees consisted predominantly of non-executive directors. In general, all the companies were prepared to alter their board procedures to comply with the spirit of the Cadbury recommendations provided that the additional cost burden was not too great. The main failure in complying with the Code of Best Practice was in only having two non-executive directors which meant that the audit committee could not have at least three non-executive directors (paragraph 4.3, p. 59).

The least frequent board meetings were held quarterly and the most frequent were held monthly. At all board meetings[2] the directors considered a range of matters which invariably include: the chief executive's report on past performance and prospects; a review of key information on all operations which will include the budget, results for the latest period and performance against budget; details of major financial and property commitments; and future strategy. Other matters regularly mentioned were: a review of share price performance and significant movements in the company's shares; any use of the company seal; acquisitions and disposals.

AUDIT COMMITTEE PRACTICES IN THE CASE STUDY COMPANIES

Six of the eight cases had a 'Cadbury style' audit committee. The remaining two cases (E and F) had the full board sit as an audit committee. With the exception of B, which had four members, all of the audit committees had three members. This reflects the influence of the Cadbury report recommendation that 'there should be a minimum of three members' (App. 4, s. 6(b), p. 69). Cadbury also recommended that 'Membership should be confined to the non-executive directors of the company' (App. 4, s. 6(b), p. 69). However, as three of the six companies had only two non-executive directors not all the companies interviewed could meet this requirement. The solution was to make up numbers by recruiting an executive director to the audit committee; a move which is consistent with the CISCO (1993, p. 7) guidelines which suggested that membership need not be confined to non-executive directors. In all the companies the members of the audit committee were appointed by the board and all the audit committees were chaired by a non-executive director. The split between executive and non-executive director members of each audit committee is shown in Table 3.6.

Other executive directors were in attendance at the audit committee

Table 3.6 The Membership of the Audit Committees

	Total	Non-executive directors	Executive directors	Title of executive director
A	3	2	1	Chairman/chief executive
B	3	3		
C	4	4		
D	3	2	1	Finance director
G	3	2	1	Technical director
H	3	3		

meetings. C had the most attendees since the finance director, chief executive and another executive director are present at audit committee meetings. At B and G the finance director is in attendance, while the finance director of H attends the meeting in his capacity as company secretary. This means that with the exception of A, which did not have a finance director, there was a finance director present at all the companies which held audit committee meetings (he was a member of the audit committee at D). As one of the interviewees commented 'there is no point in holding an audit committee meeting without having a finance director present to answer questions and discuss points'. CISCO (1993, p. 7) specifies that 'As part of the arrangements, non-executive directors should have meetings (at which the executive are not present) with the company's auditors'. This guidance was only followed by: B where the finance director withdraws for a period from each meeting in order to allow free discussion between the auditor and the non-executive directors; and G where the finance director attends as required. However at C, although historically, the executive directors have not left the audit committee, the finance director encourages a situation where the auditors can, and have in the past, requested to see the non-executive directors/audit committee chairman in private if they feel that this is necessary. Elsewhere it is deemed sufficient, given that the meeting is chaired by a non-executive director, for there to be direct contact between the non-executive directors and the auditors. All meetings of the audit committees were attended by the representatives of the group auditor in the form of the audit partner and possibly audit manager, and by the company secretary who takes minutes (for D and H, the finance director was also company secretary).

Appendix 4 of the Cadbury report (p. 69) stated that 'Audit committees should be formally constituted . . .; they should be given written terms of reference which deal adequately with their membership, authority and duties . . .'. Four of the cases formalised the committee through a constitution and terms of reference, which was approved by the board. Table 3.7 covers the contents of the constitutions and terms of reference. The responsibilities, objectives or terms of reference of all the companies were clearly adapted from Cadbury (App. 4, pp. 68–71) with only H not exhibiting all the points.

One obvious omission from the formal setting up of all the audit committees was the absence of any mention of the rotation of members or a preset length of audit committee service.

The four companies who referred to the authority of the audit committee complied with Cadbury (App. 4, p. 70) which specifies that 'The audit

Table 3.7   Contents of the Formal Constitution and Terms of Reference

Subject	Companies
Formal establishing of the committee	B, C and G
Membership	All
Non-members entitled or required to be in attendance	All
Quorum	B and C
Secretarial provision	B, C and G
Notice of meetings	G only
Responsibilities, objectives, or terms of reference	All
Authority	All
Frequency of meetings	B, C and G
Reporting procedures	All

committee should have explicit authority to investigate any matters within its terms of reference, the resources which it needs to do so, and full access to information. The committee should be able to obtain outside professional advice and if necessary to invite outsiders with relevant experience to attend meetings'. However, there were no examples of additional resources being needed or of recourse to third parties at any of the companies.

The number of meetings of the audit committee in a year varied between two and four with all companies having a meeting prior to the interim and final accounts. The length of audit committee meetings varied with the subject under consideration. Typically, the final results meeting were the longest and the scope of the audit the shortest. The meetings were relatively short as the companies reported a norm of between one and two hours and a mean duration of one and a quarter hours. Overall, this means that the average annual duration of audit committee meetings was around three and a half hours for the companies visited, a duration which is substantially less than the 6.2 hours mean annual duration for large quoted companies reported by Collier (1993, p. 81). Although to an extent this reflects the reduced complexity of the issues in smaller listed companies and a decision through a well-planned agenda to focus on key issues, there must be concern that considerable reliance is being placed on the auditors and the finance director. Concerns are reduced by the auditors' close involvement in setting of the agenda for each audit committee meeting at all but one of the companies and the presentation of a written report on the financial statement and audit concerns by the auditors in half of the companies.

The subjects dealt with by each audit committee over the year were fairly consistent. The major two meetings each year considered, respectively, the draft interim financial statements and the draft annual financial statements before their submission to the main board. In carrying out this review, the committe examined the following: major accounting problems; critical accounting decisions; the adequacy of disclosures; and major audit problems. In addition, either at these or further meetings, the audit committees considered the nature and scope of the audit, the points raised by the auditors in the management letter, action taken on management letter concerns and any major control issues.

The depth and focus of consideration given to areas by the audit committee varied, as might be anticipated given its wide remit. In general, the audit committee at each company focused at an overview level on the correctness of the accounts, the true and fair view given, and how the accounts will be perceived by users. The matters for which detailed attention was reserved were those highlighted as exceptional and worthy for discussion by the auditors or finance director.

With respect to the nomination or approval of auditors and the acceptance of the audit fee, this matter was within the scope of the audit committee but in none of the companies had there been any recent occasion when the audit fee recommended to the audit committee had been changed as a result of consideration by the audit committee. The nomination or approval of the auditor was similarly reported to the audit committee and accepted without question.

THE BACKGROUND OF THE NON-EXECUTIVE DIRECTORS ON THE AUDIT COMMITTEE

An audit committee deals with fairly technical auditing, control, accounting and disclosure issues in conjunction with advice from the auditors and the finance director or equivalent. It might reasonably be thought that the audit committee should include at least some non-executive directors with expertise or at least a background in accounting or auditing.

The cases provided a range of positions. At D, both non-executive directors had accountancy or finance backgrounds and were qualified accountants, while the non-executive directors on the audit committee of A had until recently had finance backgrounds. However, the resignation of one has led to the appointment of a director with more general business experience. The audit committee of C, G and H had non-executive directors who included at least one member with financial expertise. The four members of the audit committee of C provided a balance of finance backgrounds and wider business experience as two are qualified account-ants and two have been involved in senior positions at board level in large organisations. Similarly, in G, there was an equal split between non-executive directors with an accountancy background and those without, as one director had a finance background and the other was a lawyer. Finally both B and H lacked non-executive directors with specific accounting expertise. All the audit committee members of B had extensive business experience but none had an accounting qualification. At H, the three non-executive directors had general management experience, an engineering qualification and a city background respectively.

Discussions with the finance directors revealed mixed views about the need for an accounting qualification. The majority position was that at least one non-executive with an accounting qualification was extremely useful to provide the committee with its own source of expertise but that the presence of non-accounting members was also important for, as two of the finance directors observed, 'they ask different questions which occasionally provide new insights'. The minority opinion was that as virtually all non-executive directors would have considerable experience at a senior management position which would involve extensive exposure to accounting information, there was no need for audit committee members to have specific expertise in this area. It was also pointed out that the balance of the main board and their ability to add value to the business was the major consideration in appointing new non-executive directors and that the need for the audit committee to have specific skills would not feature high on a list of considerations.

PROCEDURES IN COMPANIES WHICH DID NOT HAVE AN AUDIT COMMITTEE

Two of the companies (E and F) did not have an audit committee which fell within the definition given in the introduction. In both cases the audit committee consisted of the full board under the chairmanship of a senior non-executive director. The approach reflects the small size of the board at these companies (five and four members, respectively), which means that an audit committee with the recommended minimum number of members would virtually constitute the full board. The practices and procedures of the full board sitting as an audit committee are closely allied to those followed when the audit committee is a subcommittee of the board. However, in neither case was the approach formalised and the time spent on audit committee business was generally less than when the audit committee was a separate subcommittee with an average annual duration of around one and a half hours. In both cases, the finance director stressed that the non-executive directors have an absolute right to request a confidential meeting in private with the auditors or any advisers if they wish, although in practice this has never been done.

AUDITOR–BOARD RELATIONSHIPS

At all the companies, except A which did not have a finance director, the group finance director was in charge of the audit of the group. The group finance director negotiated with the partner and/or senior manager of the audit firm to agree the scope of the audit and the audit fee, and the audit timetable. Negotiations take place within the framework of a formal proposal put forward by the auditors. In larger companies with a number of major subsidiaries in the UK and/or abroad the process is often more involved. For example, at B and C audit fees for each division are initially negotiated separately by divisional finance directors. However, local negotiations were subject to the group finance director agreeing the final overall fee. Alternatively, at F and G, remote locations, which were audited by local auditors, were allowed to agree their own fees subject to budget constraints. Negotiations between the group finance director and the group auditors were involved mainly with respect to the integration of their work with that of local auditors. At A, the audit fee and scope of the audit was negotiated with the managing director, and the audit timetable was agreed with the company secretary. As was discussed earlier, at all the companies with an audit committee the appointment of the auditors and the agreement of the audit fee was formalised by being considered first by the audit committee which would make a recommendation to the main board where finally approval would be given.

For the majority of companies the day-to-day running of the audit was delegated to senior finance staff at the head office, divisions or subsidiaries. For example, at F and G routine contact at head office with the auditors was delegated to the financial controller, while for divisions or subsidiaries at home and/or overseas, responsibility for the routine inter-face with the auditors was delegated to the finance director of the division or subsidiary. In addition to servicing the auditors, at the subsidiaries or divisions of all the companies it was normal practice for divisional management letters to be initially discussed at local level before being synthesised into a final management letter, which was reviewed by the head office auditors and the main board finance director.

Although none of the companies had an internal audit department, the finance departments at the various companies had responsibility for supervising remote divisions and subsidiaries. For example, at B, specific finance staff were responsible for monitoring individual subsidiaries through examining their monthly budget reports and regular visits, and the group finance director also visited the auditors in each major country at least once per year to discuss the management letter and discuss the audit in detail. The group finance directors and/or financial controllers at E, F and G regularly visit overseas subsidiaries to discuss any problems, including any highlighted by the auditors, which arise, and are 'involved' in controlling these businesses.

The use of the main board at E and F as an audit committee meant that the auditors met with the full board each year. In both cases, the time spent by the auditors with the directors is much longer than prior to the Cadbury recommendations, when the auditors attended only for the brief period when the accounts were being considered. At A, B, D and H the auditors do not attend the board meetings, even those prior to the interim and final accounts, unless specifically requested. At A, this had always been the case and it was justified by the fact that the small size of the company meant that there was close contact between the auditors and the directors. B also did not have auditors at board meetings on the grounds that the auditors attending the main board meeting as well as the audit committee was an unnecessary duplication of effort. At B and H the formation of the audit committee had led to the auditors no longer attending the board meetings at which the interim and final results were considered. The auditors of C and G briefly attend the results board meetings in order to be available to answer any matters raised by other board members.

THE OPINIONS OF FINANCE DIRECTORS

The finance directors of the companies which had formed an audit committee, with the exception of G, believed that the setting up or continued operation of the audit committee had been beneficial and had not involved any significant costs. A, B and H agreed that the audit committee had three main benefits: (1) an improvement in the non-executive directors' awareness of and involvement in the critical accounting and business issues; (2) the provision of an independent forum for meetings between the non-executive directors and the auditors which provides an opportunity for a close relationship to develop between them; and (3) enhancement of the flow of information to directors. C thought that the main benefit of the audit committee was the provision of a useful check and balance on the management decisions of executives and the finance director of D stressed the role of the audit committee in reassuring the non-executive directors that the auditors have no problems or disputes surrounding the audit and financial reports. At D, the existence of an audit committee was also seen as avoiding the auditors having to ask to see non-executive directors, as might have happened in the past if there had been a dispute (in practice this never happened). Further, from the viewpoint of the finance director the contact between the non-executive directors and the auditors has deflected some of the arguments which arose between him and the board on accounting treatments. In the past, the finance director maintained that a particular approach had to be adopted because of the auditors. Now the non-executive directors, who occasionally disbelieved this assertion, argue directly with the auditors.

G's finance director was sceptical about the audit committee and held that this committee was largely cosmetic and of little benefit to shareholders. The basis for this opinion was that the main power of the auditor lay in the threat of qualification rather than access to the non-executive directors. However, G conceded that the audit committee did have benefits for non-executive directors and auditors. For the former, it increased their knowledge of the business and gave them a degree of comfort on the accounts; while for the latter, it provided an opportunity to build a relationship with the non-executive directors who would otherwise not be known to them.

Subject to the need to employ an extra non-executive director where there were only two, the Cadbury recommendations on audit committees had limited cost implications for the companies interviewed. Since in all but one of the cases the meeting was held on the same day as the main board meeting, the additional costs of the audit committee related only to servicing the committee and the costs of the auditor in preparing for the meeting and in attending it.

Beyond audit committee considerations, the Cadbury recommendations were held by the interviewees to have imposed extra costs through the formalisation of corporate governance and the need for increased disclosure. For individual companies, the impact had been more specific. Three of the companies (B, C and H) said compliance with all or the main provisions of the Cadbury Code of Practice had not so far caused significant problems, and the interviewees had few criticisms of the recommendations. The main change in B was the considerable effort devoted to the formalisation of existing procedures in an Organisation Manual. At C, few additional costs or problems were imposed beyond restructuring the audit committee. For H, which already had well-documented procedures covering all levels of staff, the only changes were the strengthening of the non-executive directors by an additional appointment and the formation of the audit committee.

A, D and G all thought that compliance with the Cadbury Code of Practice had posed considerable problems due to the size of the company and strict cost controls. In each of the companies a decision was taken not to appoint a third non-executive director on cost and availability grounds. In A and D, the combining of the role of chairman and chief executive was deemed essential for their size of company (but both companies believed that there was currently a strong and independent element on the board). A had formed its audit committee in response to pressure from a non-executive director who represented a major shareholder, but D stated that its audit committee and remuneration committee would probably not have been set up but for Cadbury.

E and F were more critical of the Cadbury recommendations. Neither company had an audit committee as a separate sub-committee of the main board and complied only with the recommendations to the extent that they thought was sensible for companies of their size. Both companies argued that it was important for all the directors to be responsible for discharging the responsibilities of the audit committee, and that two non-executive directors were perfectly adequate representation for a company of their size. In the case of F, the role of non-executive directors has also been strengthened by their chairmanship of the remuneration and audit committees. The companies were perfectly satisfied with their modified corporate governance procedures and believed that they were well suited to their relatively straightforward businesses. The finance director of E believed that the Cadbury report failed both to specify the nature of the problems which led to it being set up and to explain how the recommendations solved the problems caused by recent financial scandals. Investors in equities and especially in smaller companies must accept that risks are involved and that structures and procedures alone will be unable to remove them. The finance director of F was similarly unclear as to how Cadbury would solve the problems of dramatic corporate failure. One weak link was deemed to be the ability of an unscrupulous dominant personality to choose directors who on paper might appear independent but who in practice were unlikely to be a check on his activities. The interviewee admitted to taking the line of least resistance on Cadbury in complying only with the essentially costless recommendations.

An area of concern for all companies was the additional costs which might arise from the requirement on directors to 'report on the effectiveness of the company's system of internal control' (Cadbury Committee, para. 4.5, p. 59). For example, B was concerned that this might force it to form an internal audit department, while C's finance director felt that the requirement could involve additional audit fees and may even necessitate the setting up of an internal audit department. In both companies, the possibility of forming an internal audit department had been considered and rejected as not being cost justified with the conclusion that internal audit would not add value to the business and would therefore weaken its competitiveness.

THE OPINIONS OF NON-EXECUTIVE DIRECTORS

Three companies provided a non-executive director who was prepared to be interviewed. The non-executive directors (denoted as X, Y and Z) had the following profiles. X had been an executive director of the company and originally had a legal background. He also had widespread experience at board level and had been a non-executive director/non-executive chairman at a number of companies. Y was chairman of the board and the audit committee. Originally he had an accountancy background. He has widespread experience at board level and is a non-executive director/non-executive chairman at a number of public and private companies. Z was on the board as a representative of a major shareholder. He had a city background and was employed by a merchant bank. He held one other non-executive directorship. All three non-executive directors were on the audit committee or quasi-audit committee.

Opinions differed as to the main role of the non-executive on the board. X believed that the role of the non-executive is to contribute to the long-run prosperity of the business to the benefit of the shareholders, employees and the wider community. To this end, protecting shareholder interests through ensuring good corporate governance was an important but not overriding objective. Y defined his role in terms of a number of functions carried out with the principal objective of 'benefiting and protecting the shareholders'. Z felt that the main role of the non-executive director was threefold: (1) to protect shareholders' interests; (2) to provide an input to the development of company strategy which was free from contact with the routine running of the company and came from experience in a different field; and (3) to widen the financial and business contacts of the company.

With respect to the non-executive's role in the corporate governance systems of the company, all the respondents indicated that the non-executive is a member of a board team, and that the non-executive directors cannot take away from executive directors their responsibility for running the business. Therefore their role is limited to ensuring that company policies are established and followed, and that the executive directors act in the interests of the shareholders within laid-down parameters. For all the non-executive directors, membership of the remuneration and audit committees was central to achieving these objectives.

The non-executive directors also stressed the importance for corporate governance of the non-executive director's role as a judge of people. The non-executive director must appraise fellow directors and professional advisers to ensure that all are careful, honest and straightforward. Z stressed that this role was especially important for him, as the roles of the chairman and chief executive were combined in his company. Z thought that in smaller companies the combination of these roles was often the most cost-effective approach. However, investors should be aware that the situation poses additional risks and expect to see adequate counter-balances in the membership of the board. Z believed that from the viewpoint of institutional investors dominant personalities on the board were the major corporate governance risk area, and of much more concern than the functioning of the audit committee. Based on his board-level experience at other companies, X warned that non-executive directors must be careful not to dominate the board and constrain the executive directors in the name of corporate governance. He suggested that it is the chairman's job to prevent this and ensure that there is a proper balance on the board.

X and Y agreed that the audit committee assisted in fulfilling their corporate governance role. X felt that the main purpose of the audit committee was to allow non-executive directors to study the company accounts to see if they 'feel correct' in the light of the information that has been given to the full board at regular meetings, and to review major

control concerns. In particular, the audit committee provides opportunities: (1) to gain additional information to which the non-executive
director might otherwise not be privy; (2) to ensure that the accounts are
not misleading; and (3) to appraise the quality and reliability of the
auditors. In contrast, Y emphasised that the major benefit of the audit
committee was that it brought the non-executive directors closer to the
auditors. This allowed them to better assess the quality of the external
auditors and was a valuable exercise in obtaining confirmation that the
group has adequate controls and that the final accounts were properly
prepared. However, Y considered that the role of the audit committee
must not be overemphasised. Z, who had experience of a Cadbury-style
audit committee at another company, felt that the full board sitting as an
audit committee was not as effective as an audit committee which was a
subcommittee of the board. In his opinion, the amount of discussion was
curtailed and the auditors were possibly more circumspect.

The non-executive directors felt that meetings of around one to two
hours for discussion of the final accounts with shorter periods for the
interim accounts and other meetings were sufficient for audit committee
meetings in smaller companies unless particular problems arose. Given
the scope of the audit committee's functions, it was deemed important that
the agenda highlighted the key areas of concern so that the meetings were
focused. The non-executive directors stated that the average time they
spent preparing for an audit committee meeting ranged from one to three
hours, although there was some variation over the year, especially between
the interim and final accounts meetings. The longest time was taken by Y,
who was the chairman of the audit committee, and might therefore be
expected to spend more time preparing. The shortest time was taken by Z,
whose company had among the shortest meetings.

The non-executive directors were uncertain as to which matters received
the greatest weight at audit committee meetings and felt that it varied
between meetings. X stated that the most important issue for the audit
committee at the latest meeting concerned some control problems at an
overseas subsidiary and the need to find reliable local accounting personnel. Y believed that at the final accounts meetings the emphasis was on
the financial statements, the accounting policies employed and the
auditors report. At other meetings the main concern tended to be control
issues. For example, a recent matter of concern was to ensure the
adequacy of treasury management procedures and policies for dealing
with an increasing volume of foreign exchange transactions. Z felt that
while the main concern at a recent meeting was the truth and fairness of

the financial statements, the majority of time was spent considering the company's corporate governance procedures.

X reported that although the finance director attends the audit committee, there is a period during the course of each meeting when he leaves to allow unhindered discussions between the auditors and non-executive directors. X believed the relationship that develops between the non-executives and the auditors is one of the major benefits of the audit committee and a period without the finance director assisted this. However, X stated that in his experience as a non-executive director this practice was an exception. Y and Z confirmed that executive directors are normally present throughout audit committee meetings and that this was essential for an audit committee to be effective. All the non-executives interviewed believed that an important feature of the audit committee is that it acts as a channel of communication between non-executive directors and the auditors.

The non-executives agreed that the essential skill for dealing with the accounting and auditing issues which might be raised at an audit committee was wide business experience. X thought that a long career in executive management was a suitable background for serving on an audit committee. However, he warned that there may be a problem where non-executives are chosen for their reputation rather than sound business background. Such figurehead directors may be ill-equipped to ensure that the executive directors are doing their job properly or contribute to the long-run prosperity of the business. In general, he believed that smaller companies rarely appointed such directors. For Y and Z, the important factor is to have a mix of expertise on the audit committee. An accountancy or finance background will assist with detailed accounting and auditing matters, but directors with other backgrounds will offer valuable alternative approaches to problems and ask different sorts of questions and add to the effectiveness of the committee.

The non-executive directors were also asked how they satisfied themselves as to the independence of the auditors. The non-executive directors generally agreed that satisfaction was achieved by a combination of the reputation of the audit firm and an assessment of the performance of the audit partner. Reputation did not extend solely to 'Big-Six' firms. Indeed, of the three companies whose non-executive directors were interviewed only G was audited by a 'Big-Six' firm, but the size of the audit firm and its ability to provide the full range of services was considered crucial and all the auditors were among the top 12 audit firms. B stressed that it was important for a group with its spread of operations for the audit firm to have an international focus as it is vital that the firm is capable of supervising the local audits of overseas companies where concepts of independence are less well developed. The non-executive directors also agreed that the audit committee, through the provision of formal regular contact with the auditors, played an important role in enabling the non-executive directors to be satisfied as to auditors' competence and reliability.

Opinions on the effectiveness of the audit committee in fulfilling the expectations of the Cadbury report were also consistent. All the non-executives interviewed thought that the spread of audit committees was a positive development. They considered that the audit committee was a useful device which provided the twin benefits of a link between the non-executive directors and the auditors and the enhancement of the information flow to non-executive directors. However, it was pointed out that the limited time devoted to audit committee meetings meant that reliance upon the audit committee to fulfil all the functions laid out in Cadbury other than at an overview level was unrealistic, and that the onus was still on the auditors to alert the directors of major areas of concern.

All the non-executive directors felt that the Cadbury recommendations were targeted at larger listed companies. X suggested that one major problem related to paragraph 2.2 of the Code of Best Practice, which states that the majority of non-executive directors should be free from any relationship that may materially interfere with the exercise of their independent judgement, apart from their fees and shareholding. Smaller listed companies generally have fewer non-executive directors on the board and therefore if any of the non-executive directors are not wholly independent, as may well be the case given the need for them to add value to the company, the board size precludes there being sufficient non-executive directors to outnumber such directors. The small board size also makes it difficult to meet set numbers of non-executive directors on the audit committee but this is probably less important. Y believed that the Cadbury recommendations involved several dangers and has undesirable consequences for all companies, especially smaller listed companies. The recommendations are bureaucratic, require non-executive directors to be responsible for things which they cannot control such as internal controls, and impose additional costs on the business mainly to the benefit of accountants. Furthermore, it is unclear how it will prevent financial scandals of the type that led to it being set up. Z felt that the important feature of the Cadbury recommendations was that they were voluntary and that only disclosure of compliance was required. Therefore investors were aware of the corporate governance system of a company and would be able to protect their interests. Z believed that the biggest risk was from a dominant personality on the board who elected 'tame' executive and non-executive directors rather than the absence of an audit committee or written board procedures.

POLICY IMPLICATIONS

The case study results discussed in this chapter have implications for the advocacy by Cadbury of a policy of the formation and effective operation of audit committees. All the companies interviewed had established an audit committee even if it did not always strictly conform to the Cadbury model, either through a failure to have a minimum membership of three non-executive directors or the presence of executive directors in the membership of the audit committee. The former shortcoming arises because five of the eight companies had five or fewer directors, including only two non-executive directors. It was felt that the need to have three non-executive directors in order to form a Cadbury-style audit committee was not a sufficient reason for incurring the costs associated with an additional non-executive director appointment. The unanimous view was that any new non-executive director must add value to the company through his business or city contacts and not be an overhead. In the latter case, executive directors in the membership reflects the CISCO suggestion for overcoming the shortage of non-executive directors by extending the membership to non-executive directors. A proposal which runs counter to the statement by Menon and Williams (1994) that for an audit committee to monitor management effectively, the non-executive membership must have a period of time with the external auditors without any executive directors being present. At only one company was this process formalised. Otherwise, although non-executive directors often had a right to ask for a private meeting with the auditors, it was the exception for the non-executives to see the auditors without an executive director being present.

The cases highlighted a possibly undesirable by-product of the Cadbury recommendations through the impact of the audit committee on contact between the auditor and the full board. The companies interviewed fell into three categories: (1) in two companies the formation of the audit committee meant that the auditors no longer attended these board meetings; (2) for another two cases the auditors had never attended the main board and did not do so when the audit committee was formed; and (3) in the remainder the auditors still attend these board meetings. In the last category are both 'board' audit committees who reported that the auditors now spend much longer with the board than prior to Cadbury recommendations. However, on balance the audit committee recommendations appears to have reduced contact between the executive directors and the auditors.

There was general support for audit committees by all but one of the finance directors interviewed. Three main benefits were consistently identified: (1) an improvement in the non-executive directors' awareness of and involvement in the critical accounting and business issues; (2) the provision of an independent forum for meetings between the non-executive directors which provides an opportunity for a close relationship to develop between the non-executive directors and the auditors; and (3) enhancement of the flow of information to directors. The negative opinion contended that the audit committee was largely cosmetic and of little benefit to shareholders. Despite this, it was conceded that the audit committee did have benefits for the non-executive directors through an improvement in their knowledge of the business and critical accounting issues, and the auditors who had the opportunity to build a relationship with the non-executive directors. Overall these benefits are more modest than those claimed in the Cadbury report (App. 4.4 (a)–(h) p. 68). Despite these positive views and a general acceptance of the need for the Cadbury recommendations among finance directors, at least two felt that the Cadbury report failed both to provide a detailed exposition of the nature of the problems which led to it being set up and to explain how the recommendations prevented financial scandals. One view was that investors in equities and especially in smaller companies must accept that risks are involved and that structures and procedures alone will be unable to remove them. It was agreed that a weakness in the proposals was the ability of an unscrupulous dominant personality to choose directors who on paper might appear independent but who in practice were unlikely to be a check on his activities. Policy makers evidently still have to persuade some directors about the wisdom of the Cadbury proposals.

The finance directors expressed general concern about the additional costs which might arise from the requirement on directors to 'report on the effectiveness of the company's system of internal control' (Cadbury Committee, paragraph 4.5, p. 59) as it was felt that this could impose significant additional costs (e.g. internal audit and accountants fees) which would not add value to the business and would therefore weaken its competitiveness.

The non-executive directors saw themselves as members of a board team and emphasised that the non-executive directors cannot take away from executive directors their responsibility for running the business. Their role is to ensure that company policies are established and followed, and that the executive directors act in the interests of the shareholders within laid-down parameters. Membership of the audit committee was central to achieving this. The interviewees also stressed the importance for corporate governance of the non-executive directors' role as a judge of people. The non-executive director must appraise fellow directors and professional advisers to ensure that all are careful, honest and straight-forward. The non-executive directors were satisfied that the time devoted to audit committee meetings at the companies was sufficient unless particular problems arose.

The non-executives agreed with the finance directors that the audit committee made them better informed and acted as a channel of communication between them and the auditors. The non-executive directors, with one exception, did not express any concern because they did not have a period alone with the external auditor, and all were agreed that the presence of the finance director was essential for an audit committee to be effective.

With respect to the skills needed by non-executive directors to serve on an audit committee, it was agreed that the essential skill for dealing with the accounting and auditing issues which might be raised was wide business experience rather than an accountancy background.

All the non-executives interviewed thought that the spread of audit committees was a positive development due to the benefits already cited. However, it was pointed out that the limited time devoted to audit committee meetings meant that reliance upon the audit committee to fulfil all the functions laid out in Cadbury other than at an overview level was unrealistic and that the onus was still on the auditors to alert the directors of major areas of concern. The non-executives felt that the Cadbury recommendations were targeted at larger listed companies. In particular, the problems in finding sufficient 'independent' non-executive directors in a small board with perhaps only two non-executive directors were not addressed. One opined that the recommendations are bureaucratic, require non-executive directors to be responsible for things which they cannot control such as internal controls, and impose additional costs on the business mainly to the benefit of accountants.

CONCLUSIONS

This chapter has shown that smaller listed companies are forming audit committees in accordance with the Cadbury recommendations. The audit committees that have been formed often fail to conform to the Cadbury guidance. In general, the divergences reflect an unwillingness to incur additional costs. Whether the audit committees that have been formed are effective is beyond the scope of this research, but certainly crucial elements proposed by Cadbury for effective audit committees are absent. For example, in a number of the cases examined the audit committee is not composed exclusively of non-executive directors, and regular meetings between the non-executive directors and the auditors without the presence of executive directors do not take place. The former situation reflects an unwillingness to bear the extra costs of more non-executive directors and difficulty with recruiting the right persons. The latter reflects either a lack of appreciation of the role of non-executive directors on audit committees or the executives' desire to maintain control.

The policy makers will need either to make the Code of Best Practice mandatory or accept this situation and incorporate modifications into the Code of Best Practice, perhaps on the CISCO lines, to reflect the different board structure in many smaller listed companies.

The opinions of the finance directors and non-executive directors on the usefulness of audit committees concur with Wolnizer (1995) that although audit committees may strengthen auditor independence and enhance public confidence in the integrity of the financial reporting process, the objective of an improvement in the quality of financial reporting is unlikely to be fulfilled. The advocates of Cadbury-style audit committees need to be careful not to claim too much.

NOTES

1. The results of t-tests and Mann–Whitney U-tests on the three variables (number of executive directors; number of non-executive directors; and number of audit committee members) revealed statistically significant differences at the 5% level between the means of the variables for the t-tests and between the values of the variables for the Mann–Whitney U-tests.
2. Due to recent financial upheavals, the focus of board meetings at H has been on fundamental policy matters and working capital forecasts rather than the monthly accounts and budgets. In practice, although such information is available to all directors for the board meeting, it is carried into working capital forecasts.

REFERENCES

Accountancy Age (1993) Pressure on Cadbury over small companies. 19 August, 3.

Bank of England (1988) Composition of company boards. *Bank of England Quarterly Bulletin*, **28**, (2), 242–5.

Bradbury, M.E. (1979) Audit Committees. *The Accountants Journal*, **58**, (12), 430–1.

Bradbury, M.E. (1990) The incentives for voluntary audit committee formation. *Journal of Accounting and Public Policy*, **9**, (1), 19–36.

Cadbury Committee (1992) *Report of the Committee on the Financial Aspects of Corporate Governance*, London: Gee & Co.

CISCO (1993) *The Financial Aspects of Corporate Governance: Guidance for Smaller Companies*, London.

Collier, P.A. (1993) Factors affecting the voluntary formation of audit committees in major UK listed companies. *Accounting and Business Research*, **23**, 91A, 421–30.

Collier, P.A. and Gregory, A. (1993) Audit committee effectiveness: an investigation of the relationship between audit committees and audit fees. Discussion Paper in Accountancy, 9019, University of Exeter.

Holland, J. (1993) Bank–corporate relations: change issues in the international enterprise. *Accounting and Business Research*, **23**, 91, 273–83.

Institute of Chartered Accountants in England and Wales (ICAEW) (1991) *Report of the Study Group on the Changing Role of the Non-Executive Director*, London.

Kaplan, R.S. (1984) The case for case studies in management accounting research. Paper presented at the American Accounting Association Annual Conference.

Kaplan, R.S. (1986). The role for empirical research in management accounting. *Accounting, Organisations and Society*, **11**, 4/5, 142–55.

Marrian, I.F.Y. (1988) *Audit Committees*, Edinburgh: ICAS.

Menon, K. and Williams, J.D. (1994) The use of audit committees for monitoring. *Journal of Accounting and Public Policy*, **13**, 121–39.

Mohr, L.G. (1985) The reliability of the case study as a source of information. In Coulam, R. and Smith, R. (eds), *Advances in Information Processing in Organisations*, Vol. 2, London: JAI Press.

Pincus, K., Rusbarsky, M. and Wong, J. (1989) Voluntary formation of corporate audit committees among NASDAQ firms. *Journal of Accounting and Public Policy*, **8**, 239–65.

Rickwood, C., Coates, J.B. and Stacy, R. (1987) Managed costs and the capture of information. *Accounting and Business Research*, **17**, 68, 319–26.

Treadway Commission (1987) *Report to the National Commission on Fraudulent Reporting*.

Wolnizer, P.W. (1995) Are audit committees red herrings? *Abacus*, **31**, 1, 45–66.

—— 4 ——

Internal Control Practices within Large UK Companies

ROGER W. MILLS

INTRODUCTION

Corporate governance is the system by which companies are governed and controlled. In Britain its roots lie in the development of public stock markets in the late nineteenth century and the need to finance the expansion of newly emerging industrial companies. The approach adopted towards corporate governance in the UK is a unitary system exemplified by a board of directors elected by the shareholders. Traditional practice is that such boards are left to their own devices but shareholders exert their views about management in a number of ways, not least of which is through the stock market by selling their shares when companies under-perform. Such action should cause the share price to fall, thereby providing feedback to company management.

During the past ten years the UK system of corporate governance has attracted considerable attention. The corporate scene of the early 1990s became associated with a number of cases of corporate mismanagement. Despite legislation in the form of the 1985, the 1989 Companies Act, the 1986 Insolvency Act (and the Insolvency Rules 1986) and the Company Directors Disqualification Act 1986, a number of unsettling corporate scandals were held to characterise the British corporate scene. The Maxwell incident which occurred in 1991 suddenly brought to a head

Corporate Governance: Responsibilities, Risks and Remuneration. Edited by Kevin Keasey and Mike Wright © 1997 John Wiley & Sons Ltd.

concern about mechanisms for controlling corporate action and particularly that of company directors. In addition, the lax accounting framework which characterised corporate UK in the 1980s and early 1990s seemed to encourage the window-dressing of company accounts, insofar as it was relatively straightforward to disguise company problems of performance and liquidity without there being any legal repercussions. At the same time, concerns arose about the role of auditors and the extent of their independence became questionable. The audit report which had been viewed as being the ultimate indicator of corporate health based upon an independent opinion on the company's affairs became the subject of much debate, particularly as regards the so-called 'expectations gap'. While auditors report to shareholders there may be an expectation that their views will be more broadly focused and there have been increasing demands for them to recognise wider interests in terms of both the interests of parties they serve and their scope.

Concerns about corporate reporting in the UK and issues of corporate governance led to demands for better accounting and auditing procedures and culminated in the setting up of the Cadbury Committee and the publication of the Cadbury Report (Cadbury Committee, 1992a). The recommendations of the Cadbury Committee on corporate governance included a Code of Best Practice with recommendations of a voluntary nature. However, institutions led by the National Association of Pension Funds, an industry group, sought to pressurise company directors to adopt the Cadbury ideas, thus making company boards more responsive to shareholders' concerns. Furthermore, sanctions have been imposed to enforce the Cadbury recommendations and since July 1993 companies listed on the London International Stock Exchange have been required to comply with these recommendations. The rationale behind the Cadbury Committee (1992) recommendations lies in:

'... Bringing clarity to the respective responsibilities of directors, shareholders, and auditors will also strengthen trust in the corporate system. Companies whose standards of corporate governance are high are the more likely to gain the confidence of investors and support for the development of their business' (1.6, p. 58).

Poor internal controls have been reckoned to contribute significantly to the cases of corporate incompetence or malpractice which have arisen and, based upon a larger research study, this chapter provides a review of alternative views about the scope and limits of internal controls and directors' responsibilities in ensuring their effectiveness.

The adequacy of a company's control system is linked in no small way to the issue of risk assessment and management—it is to avoid exposure to major business risks that companies typically pay considerable attention to internal control systems. This chapter considers this related issue of risk assessment and, following a review of the internal controls issue, it considers approaches adopted by companies for assessing and managing important potential business risks. A description of the research study, the results and a conclusion summarising the main findings and their implications are also provided.

THE INTERNAL CONTROLS ISSUE

In this section a review of recent developments relating to the internal controls issue and risk assessment is provided prior to a description of the results of the study of practices within large UK companies.

The Cadbury Report considers that all directors, whether or not they have executive responsibilities, should be responsible for ensuring that 'the necessary controls over the activities of their companies are in place and working' (Code of Best Practice, 1.8, p. 58). It also underlines the view that the board of directors is responsible for the governance of companies. These responsibilities include the company's strategic aims, providing the leadership to put them into effect, supervising the management of the business and reporting to shareholders on their stewardship. As a result, the Code of Best Practice requires directors to include a report in their annual report 'on the effectiveness of the company's system of internal control' (Code of Best Practice, 4.5, p. 59).

Following the publication of the Code of Best Practice by the Cadbury Committee, a Working Group consisting of accountancy professionals and practitioners was set up. Its objectives were to develop a set of criteria for assessing effectiveness and to develop guidance for companies on the form in which directors should report. In October 1993 it published draft guidance relating to internal controls and financial reporting for directors of listed companies which drew heavily on the work published in the USA by the Treadway Commission (COSO, 1992).

This draft guidance was revised a year later by the same Working Group. The revamped draft was reduced to a statement of principles rather than a lengthy and complicated set of detailed guidelines which did not require directors to report on the effectiveness of the internal control system. A critical issue was the definition and scope of internal controls and that adopted by COSO (1992) was drawn upon heavily by the Working Group when producing the draft guidance. This definition identifies three organisational objectives against which an company can be assessed in terms of whether it is meeting these requirements:

> 'Internal control is a process, effected by an entity's board of directors, management and other personnel, designed to provide reasonable assurance regarding the achievement of objectives in the following categories—effectiveness and efficiency of operations, reliability of financial reporting, and compliance with applicable laws and regulations' (Cadbury Committee Working Group, 1993).

Within this definition internal control is viewed as a process, not merely an event. It is a series of occurrences that permeate an entity's activities. Internal controls should, therefore, be embedded in the entity's activities rather than run parallel to the operating activities. Furthermore, according to COSO (1992) the more these (internal) controls can be integrated with the company's management systems, the more they help to provide quality control, prevent unnecessary costs and protect the company against unwelcome surprises. However, this attention to systems should not ignore that the human resource element has an important part to play in the effectiveness of internal controls. While the board of directors is responsible for establishing the strategic objectives of the firm, these can only be accomplished by people who work within the company. What is more, no matter how well developed, an internal control system can only provide reasonable assurances about whether a company's objectives are being achieved and it is important to realise that any system has its limitations.

The Working Group limited directors' reporting responsibilities to internal financial controls, which are those established to provide reasonable assurance of the maintenance of proper accounting records and the reliability of financial information used within the business or for publication. This definition was further supported in the guidance published by the Working Group in December 1994, which defined internal financial control as being the establishment of internal controls:

> '... in order to provide reasonable assurance of: (a) the safeguarding of assets against use or disposition; and (b) the maintenance of proper accounting records and the reliability of financial information used within the business or for publication.'

Whereas the COSO (1992) definition viewed the internal control system as an integrated framework which ties both financial and operational controls together, the Working Party focused attention upon internal financial controls:

> 'In principle, the definition of internal financial control excludes efficiency, value for money, and legal and regulatory compliance issues. In practice, however, consideration of the effectiveness of internal financial control may need to include the consideration of certain operational controls which address activities which have or could have a potentially material financial impact on the true and fair view presented in the financial statements' (Cadbury Committee Working Group, 1994, Para. 10).

One recommendation arising out of Cadbury's Code of Best Practice, and implemented in the reporting and controls requirements, is that directors should make a statement in the annual report about 'the effectiveness of the system of internal control, and that the auditors should report thereon' (4.5, p. 59). In fact, effectiveness is a thorny issue, but a useful contribution to its interpretation within the context of the internal control system was provided by COSO (1992). According to COSO internal control consists of the interrelated components illustrated in Figure 4.1. At the base of the figure is the control environment that serves as the foundation for internal control and which is intended to provide an atmosphere in which people conduct their activities and carry out their control responsibilities. Within the control environment the board of directors should assess the risk of the specified objectives and, in particular, the effectiveness and efficiency of operations, the reliability of financial reporting and compliance with applicable laws and regulations. Having assessed the risk, the next step is to implement control activities which represent the policies and procedures to ensure that management directives to address risk are carried out. This whole process needs to be closely monitored with any corrective action being taken as the need arises. Furthermore, during the whole process, information needs to be gathered and communicated in all directions.

The COSO framework can be extended into a three-dimensional format

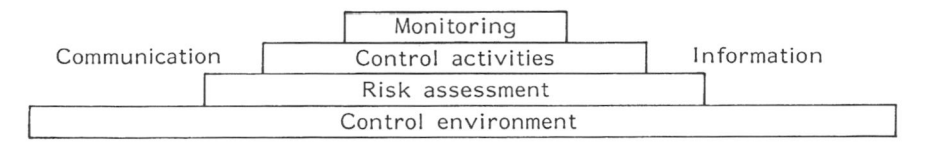

Figure 4.1   The COSO Framework for Internal Control

as illustrated in Figure 4.2. On the face of the figure five rows represent the elements of internal control discussed with reference to Figure 4.1, i.e. Monitoring and corrective action, Information and communication, Control activities, Risk assessment, Control environment. Activities are represented by the vertical columns at the side of the figure (A1, A2, A3) and objectives are represented on the top of the figure (Operations, Financial reporting, Compliance). There is a direct relationship between objectives, which are what a company strives to achieve; the elements which represent what is needed to achieve the objectives; and activities. In principle, the effectiveness of an internal control system can be assessed in terms of whether each of these three objectives is functioning properly by activity and according to the elements of control.

The criteria for assessing the effectiveness of internal controls produced by the Working Group (1994) were identified within the headings of the COSO approach (see Appendix), but it was recognised that the definition of effectiveness is in reality a potentially thorny issue. For example, in a discussion paper, the Auditing Practices Board (1995) stated that:

'Although criteria for assessing effectiveness have been established by the Working Group, parameters have yet to be established on what is meant by 'effective' . . .. Effectiveness is a matter of judgement and there are no absolutes; one board of directors may design a control structure that they consider appropriate although others may judge the structure as being a limiting factor to the company's ability to create wealth.'

Apart from the technical issues associated with internal control systems, it has to be recognised that they will often have limitations, no matter how

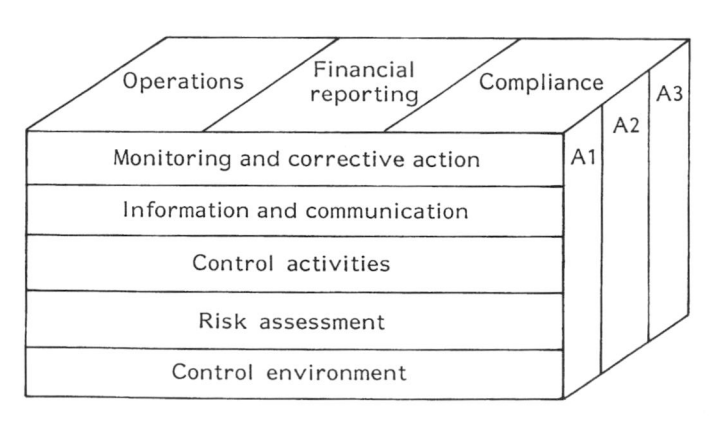

Figure 4.2 Extended COSO Framework

well designed and operated, arising from many potential sources. Not least of these is poor human judgement in decision making and, within the context of human judgement, the role of the finance function and non-executive directors is important. Finance directors and their staff play a significant part because they are involved in developing corporate-wide budgets and plans, tracking and analysing financial performance, and with many operational and compliance issues. Furthermore, their responsibilities extend not only to the company as a whole but also to its subsidiaries.

The role of the finance director is particularly important and can be seen as having both an internal and an external dimension. Internally the finance director is a facilitator to the main board and externally he or she represents a link with the markets, suppliers and clients of the company (Bruce, 1994). A board of directors may at times have to be led by the expertise and recommendations of the finance director both in terms of purely financial matters and also on matters of corporate governance. In terms of internal control the finance director plays a critical role and this will often also be so for risk analysis where he or she is often in the best position to be able to assess how badly the company would be effected under the worst possible scenario. This means that the finance director can provide valuable input upon required monitoring and follow-up procedures.

One other important human component of the internal control process is the non-executive director. Historically, the role of the non-executive director has been primarily of an advisory nature, often being appointed on the recommendation of the chairman or one of the other directors. The UK corporate governance initiatives has emphasised the important contribution of the non-executive. One important contribution identified for non-executives by the Cadbury Report was in relation to the audit committee: 'The board should establish an audit committee of at least three non-executive directors with written terms of reference which deal clearly with its authority and duties' (Code of Practice, 4.3). The function of the audit committee is to provide a link between the board of directors and the auditors that is independent of the company's management and which is responsible for the company's accounting system. It was intended that such a committee would be formed wholly of non-executive directors, but concern was expressed that the exclusion of executives might not be wholly appropriate. As a consequence, the Cadbury Report recommended that any board member should be allowed to attend meetings of the audit committee.

The adoption of audit committees by UK companies has been influenced by North American practice where such committees have long been established. Audit committees in the USA are a requirement for listing on the New York Stock Exchange and in Canada are a legal requirement. In the USA and Canada it is the non-executive directors who form the majority, unlike the UK where boards tend to have a majority of executive directors. Furthermore, in the USA the issue of non-executive directors' independence is seen as being critical and they are supposed to be free from any relationship, financial or otherwise, which might interfere with the exercise of independent judgement and be able to resign if necessary from the directorship without financial hardship.

The case has been made in the USA for extending the traditional role of the audit committee to include a periodic review of the company's risk assessment process and to consider significant financial and non-financial risks. Such a risk management audit would require material risks facing the company to be identified and analysed, the company's efforts to control these risks to be examined, a comparison of the risks and company responses, and the recommendation of improvements in company activities in the identification, control and financing of critical risks.

Risk affects a company's ability to survive, compete successfully within its industry, conserve its financial strength and a positive public image, and maintain the overall quality of its products, services and people (COSO, 1992). A key issue in the assessment of risk relates to the definition used. For example, COSO defines risk assessment as 'the identification and analysis of relevant risks to achievement of the objectives forming a basis for determining how the risks should be managed' (p. 29).

Risk can be expressed in terms of some exposure to potential loss which is significant and capable of being identified and controlled by management. In a research report by the Canadian Institute of Chartered Accountants, Boritz (1990) offered a working definition of a firm's risk as being 'the possibility of loss as a result of the combination of uncertainty and exposure flowing from investment decisions or commitments'. In terms of risk measurement there are different views. For example, according to Boritz (1990), the expected loss at any point in time is the sum across all exposure categories of the exposure amounts multiplied by the probabilities that will lead to the actual loss. Effective risk management strategies and techniques can reduce the possibility of such loss to an acceptable level. In principle, good risk management can ensure that earnings and assets are protected and in terms of top management action the integration of risk management with corporate strategy can be particularly important (Ealy, 1993).

To be most effective, risk assessment and management should be directed below the entity as a whole (business unit activity level). Dealing with risks at this level helps to focus attention and risk assessment upon major business units or functions such as sales, production, marketing, technology development and research and development. COSO (1992) based risk assessment and management on Porter's Five Forces and Value Chain Analysis. It recognised that risk can arise at the entity-wide or activity level. From an entity-wide perspective risk can arise from external and internal factors. Examples of external factors are technology development, a change in customer needs and expectations, competition, new legislation, natural catastrophes and economic changes. Examples of internal factors are the disruption of information systems, the quality of personnel hired, a change in management responsibilities, the misappropriation of the company's resources and an unassertive or ineffective board or audit committee.

The Cadbury Code of Best Practice (Cadbury Committee, 1992b) focused attention upon the importance of risk assessment, management and the internal control system and was supported by the Guidance for Directors (Cadbury Committee, 1994). This suggested that the extent and formality of individual internal financial controls should have regard to the materiality of the financial risks being incurred, the likelihood of such risks crystallising, and cost/benefit issues. In the Guidance on *Going Concern and Financial Reporting* (1994) the Working Group also recognised that risks need to be identified and managed. However, the Guidance included not only financial risks but also other risks which could affect the company's future as a going concern. To achieve this it proposed that directors should assess sensitive past events and the effects in the eventuality of a recurrence. Furthermore, they should be constantly aware of the external environment in which the company is operating. Factors which directors may take into account when assessing such other risks include consistency of earnings; stability of the cost base; recurring operating losses; fluctuating operating profits and losses; arrears of dividends; current dividends being paid out of retained rather than current earnings; non-compliance with statutory capital requirements; work stoppages or other labour difficulties; loss of key management or staff; loss of a key patent or franchise; high levels of stock which may include obsolete stock; long-overdue debtors; potential losses from long-term contracts; continuing to use old fixed assets because there are no funds to replace them; adequacy of the company's insurance policies; and signs that the company may be overtrading.

THE RESEARCH STUDY AND RESULTS

Research Study

The study was undertaken between 1 February 1994 and 31 March 1995, its purpose being to research internal control practices within large UK companies. It was directed at senior accountancy and audit professionals, finance directors and non-executive directors.

Data were collected primarily through a questionnaire which was pilot-tested with directors from four large companies. The research study sample consisted of finance directors from the top 100 companies in terms of market capitalisation as quoted on the London International Stock Exchange in February 1994. The 68 replies received represented a response rate of 68%. Of these replies, 52 were usable, resulting in a usable response rate of 52%.

Data from auditors and non-executive directors were collected primarily through structured interviews. As regards the auditors, the views of partners in major audit firms were sought. In the case of non-executive directors, the interviews with finance directors established non-executive directorships held by interviewees. Those finance directors holding non-executive directorships were interviewed about their views from this perspective. In addition, non-executive directors from ten companies within the sample were approached to elicit their views. Questionnaire response rates are summarised in Table 4.1. A breakdown of respondents by position in the company is provided in Table 4.2.

Research Study Results

(a) Internal Controls

One recommendation arising out of Cadbury's Code of Best Practice and implemented in the reporting and controls requirements is that directors should make a statement in the annual report about the effectiveness of the system of internal control. Respondents were asked about the exten-siveness of their reporting, whether they reported on internal controls which include financial controls only, or whether their reporting also

Table 4.1 Questionnaire Response Rate

	No. of companies
Questionnaire completed and interview conducted	16
Questionnaire completed, no interview conducted	36
Company policy not to take part in surveys	16
Not willing to participate	32
Total	100

Table 4.2 Respondent Breakdown by Position in the Company

	Number	%
Finance Director	40	76.9
Audit Director	1	1.9
Finance and Control Director	1	1.9
Group Internal Auditor	7	13.6
Group Chief Accountant	2	3.8
General Manager	1	1.9
	52[a]	100

[a]The analysis conducted throughout the report is based on the 52 company representatives who responded to the questionnaire or participated in the interviews.

includes operational controls. Most respondents (76.9%) replied that their internal controls were not restricted to financial ones. The main reason given for this was that directors are responsible not only for the publication of the financial statements but also for the company's management systems which included operational controls. The respondents were also asked about their personal views on the matter and most (76.9%) responded that internal controls should not be restricted to financial controls but should be considered in their widest sense.

The study also sought to establish how companies interpreted the effectiveness of internal controls. The responses in Table 4.3 illustrate that 31% of respondents linked the issue of effectiveness with aspects of financial reporting as suggested by the Guidance for Directors (1994) and 27.7% of the respondents interpreted effectiveness in terms not only of effective financial controls but also of business (operational) controls.

In many companies, the responsibility for ensuring effectiveness is most likely to lie in the hands of the internal audit function. In view of the

Table 4.3   Interpretation of Effectiveness

Interpretations of effectiveness	%
Proper and timely accounting records are maintained	31.0
Effective financial and business controls	27.7
Risk of material loss	13.8
Capital adequacy	13.8
Reasonable assurance that company's assets are safeguarded	6.9
Achieving the objectives of the operations of company concerned	3.4
Open reporting to shareholders	3.4
Total	100.0

importance the internal audit function has received since the publication of the Cadbury Report, attention was given to structure and characteristics of the internal audit function in this research study.

Most of the respondent companies (92.3%) were found to have an internal audit function and Table 4.4 shows that in most cases the audit function had been in existence for 5 years or more prior to 1990. As regards the size of the audit function, the majority of respondent companies had a department of up to twenty people, but the range in sizes was substantial, as illustrated in Table 4.5.

Statistical analysis was undertaken to test whether a relationship existed between the size of the audit function and the size of the company in terms of turnover, profit before interest and tax, capital employed and the total number of employees. No statistically significant relationship was found to exist with any of the measures of size tested.

The study also considered to whom the internal audit function reported

Table 4.4   Number of Years Audit Function has been Established

No. of years internal audit function has been established	Frequency (%)	Cumulative frequency (%)
1	8.3	8.3
5	12.5	20.8
10	29.2	50.0
15	8.3	58.3
20	16.7	75.0
25 and more	25.0	100
Total	100	

Table 4.5   Size of Audit Function

Size of audit function (no. of individuals involved)	%
Up to 10	29.2
Between 11 and 20	20.9
Between 21 and 30	8.3
Between 31 and 40	8.3
Between 41 and 50	8.3
Between 51 and 100	12.5
More than 100	12.5
Total	100.0

and the responses are summarised in Table 4.6. In the majority of cases, reporting is to the finance director and the audit committee. It was rare for the reporting to be to the audit committee only and even rarer for the internal audit function to report directly to the main board of directors.

In addition to questions about the audit function, this study investigated the role of the finance director as a consequence of the Cadbury Report and the nature and characteristics of the audit committee. Most finance directors (76.9%) felt that their role had not changed as a result of Cadbury, and all companies which participated in the study had an audit committee made up entirely of non-executive directors, with the number of non-executive directors forming the audit committee ranging between three and nine people. Statistical testing showed there to be no significant relationship between company size and the size of the audit committee.

The duties of the audit committee provided by this study were found to include recommending to the board the appointment of the external auditor and the audit fee, reviewing both interim and annual financial statements prior to board review, setting the nature and scope of the audit with the external auditor, and reviewing internal control systems.

Table 4.6   Audit Function Reporting

Internal audit function reports to	%
The main board of directors	8.3
Finance director only	29.2
Audit committee only	12.5
Finance director and audit committee	50
Total	100

(b)   Risk Assessment

The study sought to identify how companies define and assess business risk. From the summary responses shown in Table 4.7, it can be seen that the effect upon operational or financial stability and shareholders' funds featured as being particularly important.

Risk assessment and its management was a particular area of attention in the follow-up interviews. As a consequence of these interviews, the framework illustrated in Figure 4.3 for assessing and managing risk was found to be appropriate and is consistent with the approach developed by COSO (1992).

The starting point in risk assessment and management is the identification of key risks. In fact, the risks that specific companies have to manage may often be directly identifiable with the type of industry in which they operate. For example, in pharmaceutical companies product quality risks and failure in the areas of research and development can prove to be particularly detrimental. On the other hand, in banks counterparty credit risk, liquidity and operational risks are typically a top priority when analysing important potential business risks.

Table 4.7   Risk Definition

Risk definitions provided by respondents	%
Events or occurrences which may have a significant effect on the operational or financial stability of the group	56.6
Issues which, if not carefully managed, would be detrimental to shareholders' funds	20.1
Security of assets	6.7
Product quality and availability	6.7
Exposures to adverse impact on R&D capabilities	3.3
Market penetration and share	3.3
Information and intellectual property	3.3
Total	100

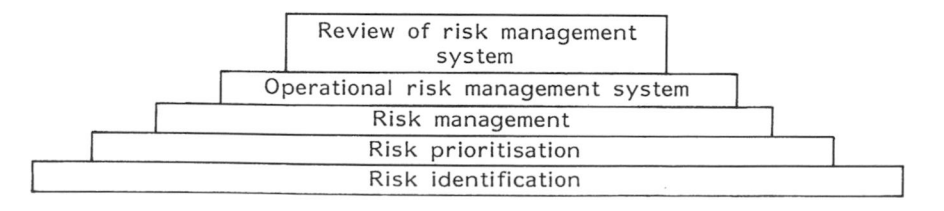

Figure 4.3   Risk Assessment and Management Framework

Risk prioritisation goes hand in hand with identification. It is important to prioritise major risks because it is difficult and not necessarily sensible to attempt to control all risks. There is a fine balance between quantity and quality which is often well expressed in terms of the Pareto principle—control of the 20% of the risks which impact most upon 80% of the business. With this in mind there are two important criteria for identifying those high-priority risks—the significance of impact upon future profits and cash flows and the likelihood of occurrence. These two are consistent with findings from the main part of the study in which respondent companies were found to be most concerned with risks which would impact upon immediate profitability and cash flow. In fact, greater concern was shown with short-term factors, and longer-term strategic issues were seen as being less important. This is consistent with an earlier study which identified a managerial focus upon the short term rather than the long term (Marsh, 1991).

Risk identification applies not only to the company as a whole but also to each operating unit, segment, division, activity or subsidiary. It is also more useful when undertaken for parts of the business because risk control is often more easily achieved at business unit level. To facilitate risk prioritisation by managers for parts of the business the matrix illustrated in Figure 4.4 captures the type of thinking found to be used. The vertical axis represents the significance of impact on profitability and cash flows while the horizontal axis represents the probability of occurrence. The shaded area is the most critical to understand and control and corresponds with high significance in terms of impact upon profitability and cash flows and a high probability of occurrence.

Given a high probability of occurrence, the shaded area is often more

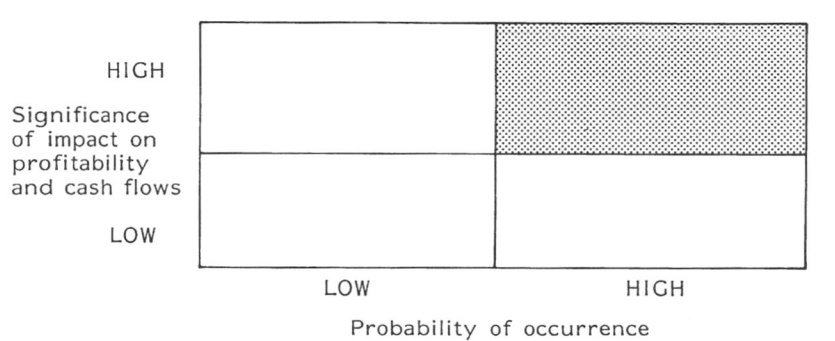

Figure 4.4 Risk Prioritisation Framework

straightforward than the area represented by the top left-hand quadrant. This quadrant typically includes just the type of issues that are often unexpected, difficult to identify and, therefore, difficult to prioritise. A good example of such a risk is information system sabotage in a bank. The probability of occurrence may be low but the significance of impact could be very high in terms of widespread disruption to operations which would affect profits and cash flow.

The prioritisation of risk was investigated as part of the study. The results revealed that most (61.5%) of the responding companies have a process for prioritising risks facing the company. When questions about how risks are prioritised were raised in face-to-face interviews, a number of common issues emerged relating to the financial impact, experience, risk audits and the importance of a strategic review.

As regards risk management, all 52 responding companies were found to have adopted the Cadbury recommendations and risk management is regarded as an essential activity. Risk management requires the identification of ways to minimise the probability of occurrence. In many cases the ways used were typically unique to individual companies as illustrated by the summary of responses in Table 4.8.

The development of an appropriate operational risk management system is vital and it is here that the link with the internal control process is important. A key challenge recognised by interviewees is to devise a system for controlling risks which not only recognises their potentially important individual impact upon the business, but also a sound review process so that the system is evaluated in terms of its effectiveness in preventing risks from occurring.

CONCLUSION

This chapter has provided a review of literature and summarised the results of part of a larger study concerning internal control practices within large UK companies. Recognising also that the adequacy of a company's control system is linked in no small way to the issue of risk assessment and management, this chapter has considered risk assessment and has reviewed approaches adopted by companies for assessing and managing important potential business risks. The main results indicate that (1) most companies include operational controls in their definition of internal control, a practice supported by the personal opinion of interviewees who see no really clear distinction between the operational and

Table 4.8   Risk Management Methods Used

Risk management methods used by respondents	%
Allocation of responsibility for specific risks to appropriate line and functional directors/executives, co-ordinating committees and project teams	22.6
Review of control environment of the company	19.4
Expenditure limits	6.6
Identification, reduction through managerial actions, contingency planning and insurance	9.8
Regular main board reviews to assess developments and continue to estimate likelihood of potential outcomes	6.4
Use of established management procedures and risk management functions involving reporting to a risk review committee consisting of non-executive directors	3.2
Strategic spreading of business geographically and by business stream	3.2
Pursuit of practical recommendations in audit reports	3.2
Via executive committees and asset and liabilities committees	3.2
Review of the effects of government legislation and the likely impact of economic factors	3.2
Ongoing reviews by senior finance managers with support from operational managers	3.2
Joint venture activities	3.2
Hedging policies	3.2
Contractual terms	3.2
Via contingency planning	3.2
Operationally with on-line telemetry monitoring systems	3.2
Total	100

financial controls; (2) the effectiveness of the internal control system seems to be a controversial issue with various perceptions of effectiveness being identified; and (3) risk is an important issue for which companies have developed approaches to facilitate its identification, prioritisation and management.

The results of the study in many respects are consistent with others. For example, KPMG (1996) recently reported its experience of 66 companies, varying in size from FT-SE 100 groups down to smaller listed and USM companies. In terms of reviewing internal controls, its study confirms that clients are taking the review seriously. A significant number of companies were found to be using a formal approach to risk assessment. In those corresponding with best practice, risk identification and control is con- sidered fundamental to managing the business, with (1) the aim being to identify uncontrolled risks; (2) a Business Risk Review (BRR) being carried out at both group and operating unit level including operational and compliance risks, (3) BRR being used to drive control evaluation and as a tool to monitor business risk and (4) with risks identified by lower levels of management being discussed openly and not ignored.

Many of the initiatives for developing corporate governance practices in the UK have relied upon the USA as a source of guidance, but it is important to note some cautionary observations that have been expressed about corporate USA. Bhide (1994) has argued that while US securities regulations protect investors and enhance market liquidity, they may well alienate managers and shareholders. While US rules protecting investors may be the most comprehensive and well enforced in the world, they may drive a wedge between shareholders and managers, with the result being diffuse, arm's-length shareholdings rather than long-term shareholders who concentrate their holdings in a few companies. Furthermore, Bhide argues that the system does not encourage informed oversight and counsel. He cites examples of the benefit of close manager–shareholder relationships and argues that to make truly fair evaluations, shareholders must maintain a candid, ongoing dialogue with managers. This, of course, is difficult to achieve where the fabric of the system prevents particularly close contact between shareholders and managers. He makes the case for reforming the existing system and the need for insider shareholders. Attempts to reform the system by way of reporting strategic data as well as financial data to compensate for a short-termist perspective, Bhide sees as being no solution at all.

One of the issues discussed by Bhide concerning the potential lack of informed oversight and counsel has been raised in discussions about the role of non-executive directors. There is a view that they can be used to good effect to provide some of the interface between the shareholders and management that is being called for. In fact, a pilot study by McNulty and Pettigrew (1995) forming part of wider research, based on a sample of non-executive directors from the top 200 UK industrial companies and the top 50 financial institutions, suggested that there is a trend towards their being used in such a way. McNulty and Pettigrew assert that there has been a perceptible tilt towards what they call the 'maximalist' board, typified by companies whose chairman or chief executive is the main boardroom 'shaper' and whose small but carefully chosen group of non-executive directors work well together as a team. Such non-executives are generally powerful figures and familiar with the relevant business and sector. They are allowed, indeed encouraged, to roam beyond the boardroom and develop informal information networks as part of developing a role. The board process of which they are a part ensures that agenda items encourage discussion rather than a one-way report back by the full-time executives. A similar view of the potential role of non-executive directors has been provided by Firstenberg and Malkiel (1994) with reference to the US system of corporate governance.

As a final note, there is a positive side to corporate governance which it is all too easy to lose sight. Risk aversion is not about the be-all and end-all of corporate life. Somehow corporations have to be managed in such a way that risks can be assessed in the face of what are seen to be potentially sound opportunities if value is to be created. The ultimate objective of a corporation is typically considered to be the maximisation of shareholder value. Approaches for achieving such an objective are now well developed under different brand labels and are being implemented by a growing number of corporations. The advantage of such approaches is that by drawing upon financial and strategic thinking it is possible to develop a holistic perspective of a corporation which can be analysed by business unit and principal line of business (Mills, 1994). In fact, many of the issues raised in this chapter can be seen in a positive vein because a value-creation framework may offer much potential for drawing together many key corporate governance issues from a holistic perspective. The way this may be achieved is by extending the risk management framework outlined earlier as illustrated in Figure 4.5.

APPENDIX: CRITERIA FOR ASSESSING THE EFFECTIVENESS OF INTERNAL CONTROLS

1. Control environment
   - A commitment by directors, management and employees to competence and integrity.
   - The communication of ethical values and control consciousness to managers and employees, through written codes of conduct, formal standards of discipline, and performance appraisal.
   - An appropriate organisational structure within which business can be planned, executed and controlled to achieve the objectives of the company.
   - The appropriate delegation of authority with accountability which has regard to acceptable levels of risk.
   - A professional approach to financial reporting which complies with generally accepted accounting practice.
2. Identification and evaluation of risks and control objectives

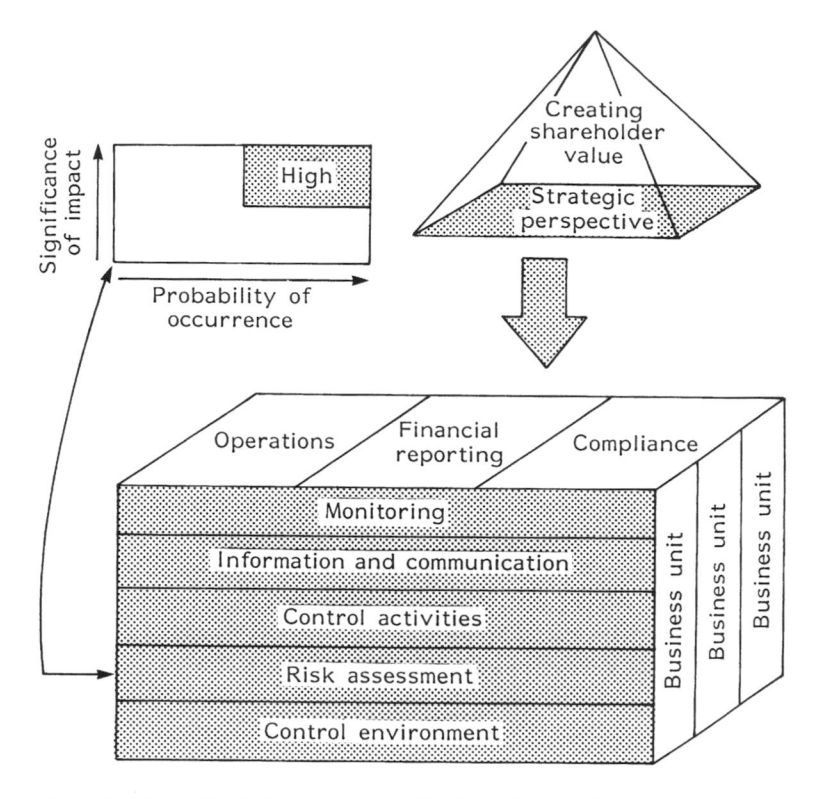

Figure 4.5   Linking Risk Assessment with Shareholder Value

- The identification of key business risks in a timely manner.
- The consideration of the likelihood of risks crystallising and the significance of the consequent financial impact on the business.
- The establishment of priorities for the allocation of resources available for control and the setting and communicating of clear control objectives.

3. Information and communication
   - Performance indicators which allow management to monitor the key business and financial activities and risks, and the progress towards financial objectives and to identify developments which require intervention (e.g. forecasts and budgets).
   - Information systems which provide ongoing identification and capture of relevant, reliable and up-to-date financial and other information from internal and external souces (e.g. monthly management accounts, including earnings, cash flow and balance sheet reporting).
   - Systems which communicate relevant information to the right people at the right frequency and time in a format which exposes significant variances from the budgets and forecasts and allows prompt

response.
4. Control procedures
   - Procedures to ensure complete and accurate accounting for financial transactions.
   - Appropriate authorisation limits for transactions that reasonably limit the company's exposure.
   - Procedures to ensure the reliability of data processing and information reports generated.
   - Controls that limit exposure to loss of assets/records or to fraud (e.g. physical controls, segregation of duties).
   - Routine and surprise checks which provide effective supervision of control activities.
   - Procedures to ensure compliance with laws and regulations that have significant implications.
5. Monitoring and corrective action
   - A monitoring process which provides reasonable assurance to the board that there are appropriate control procedures in place for all the company's financially significant business activities and that these procedures are being followed.
   - Identification of changes in the business and its environment which may require changes to the system of internal financial control.
   - Formal procedures for reporting weaknesses and for ensuring appropriate corrective action.
   - The provision of adequate support for public statements by the directors on internal control or internal financial control.

REFERENCES

Acher, G. (1994) Closing the expectations gap. *The Times* (UK), 10 November.

Auditing Practices Board (1994) The Going Concern Basis in Financial Statements, *Statement of Auditing Standards 130*, November.

Auditing Practices Board (1995) Internal financial control effectiveness. Discussion Paper, April.

Bannock Graham & Partners (1993) *Risk Management—A Boardroom Issue for the 1990s*, Sedgwick Group Development Council.

Bell, D.E. (1992) Don't put your competitive advantage at risk. *Risk Management Reports*, May/June.

Bhide, A. (1994) Deficient governance. *Harvard Business Review*, November–December.

Boritz, J.E. (1990) *Approaches to Dealing with Risk and Uncertainty*, Toronto: Canadian Institute of Chartered Accountants.

Boyd, M. (1994) Dipping into Cadbury's second layer. *Accountancy*, December.

Bruce, P. (1994) The changing role of the finance director: from passive to active. *Accountancy Age*, 1 December.

Cadbury Committee (1992a) *Report on the Committee on the Financial Aspects of Corporate Governance*, December, London: Gee & Co.

Cadbury Committee (1992b) *The Financial Aspects of Corporate Governance*, The Code of Best Practice, UK.

Cadbury Committee Working Group (1993) *Internal Control and Financial Reporting*, Draft guidance for directors of listed companies developed in response to the recommendations of the Cadbury Committee, October.

Cadbury Committee (1994) *Going Concern and Financial Reporting*, Guidance for Directors of Listed Companies registered in the UK, November.

Cadbury Committee Working Group (1994) *Internal Control and Financial Reporting*, Guidance for directors of listed companies registered in the UK, December.

Collis, D. (1992) The strategic management of uncertainty. *European Management Journal*, **10**, No. 2, June.

Committee of Sponsoring Organisations of the Treadway Commission (COSO) (1992) *Internal Control—Integrated Framework*, September.

Corrin, J. (1993) A blatant slur on executive directors' integrity. *Accountancy*, April.

DeBono, J.D. (1995) *UK Corporate Governance, Internal Control, Risk and Responsibilities*, unpublished MBA dissertation, Henley Management College, UK, January.

Ealy, T. (1993) Integrating risk management strategy with corporate strategy. *Risk Management*, April.

Fisher, A. (1995) Cracks around the edges. *Financial Times*, 27 February.

Firstenberg, P.B. and Malkiel, B.G. (1994) The twenty-first century boardroom: who will be in charge? *Sloan Management Review*, Fall.

Institute of Chartered Accountants in England and Wales (1990) *Managing Business Risk*, A statement issued as guidance to good practice.

Institute of Chartered Accountants of Scotland, Working Party (1992) *Corporate Governance*, Directors' responsibilities for financial statements.

Institute of Directors (1990) *Guidelines for Directors*, UK.

KPMG (1996) Best practice in reviewing internal control. *Financial Reporting Update*, March.

Marsh, P. (1991) Short-termism on trial. Institutional Fund Managers Association.

McNulty, T. and Pettigrew, A. (1995) Centre for Corporate Strategy and Change, Warwick Business School, University of Warwick, Coventry, CV4 7AL.

Mills, R.W. (1993) The financial aspects of corporate governance and the new era of the audit. *Journal of General Management*, Henley Management College, UK, September.

Mills, R.W. (1994) *Finance, Strategy and Strategic Value Analysis: Linking two key business issues*, Mars Business Associates Ltd.

Mills, R.W. and Weinstein, W.L. (1996) Calculating shareholder value in a turbulent environment. *Long Range Planning*, February.

Porter, M.E. (1992) Capital disadvantage: America's failing capital investment system. *Harvard Business Review*, September–October.

Reay, C. (1994) Non-executives and the expectations gap. *Accountancy*, September.

Taylor, B. and Stiles, P. (1993) Benchmarking corporate governance: the impact of the Cadbury Code. *Long Range Planning*, **26**.

Useem, M., Bowman, E., Myatt, J. and Irvine, C. (1993) US institutional investors look at corporate governance in the 1990s. *European Management Journal*, **11**, Issue 2, June.

Verschoor, C.C. (1993) UK expands role of audit committees. *Management Accounting*, December.

5

Investors' Voting Rights

CHRISTINE A. MALLIN

INTRODUCTION

The Cadbury Committee viewed institutional investors as having a special
responsibility to try to ensure that its recommendations were adopted by
companies, and also recommended that institutional investors should
disclose their policies on the use of voting rights. The institutional
investors' own representative groups are in favour of them voting
wherever possible, and indeed voting could be viewed as part of the
prudent investment principle. Institutional investors are estimated to own
between 65% and 75% of shares of quoted companies in the UK (CSO,
1994). Such concentrations of ownership tend to put institutional investors
in a different position from individual shareholders: they have access to
management in a way that individual shareholders do not, and they will
tend to have more of a say in company policies. Institutional investors
have the potential to exert significant influence on companies via their
voting rights, and this has clear implications for corporate governance,
especially in terms of the standards of corporate governance and issues
concerned with enforcement. In the Cadbury Report (Cadbury Committee, 1992) it was stated that 'Given the weight of their votes, the way in
which institutional shareholders use their power to influence the standards
of corporate governance is of fundamental importance' (paragraph 6.10).
    In this chapter the research undertaken is of an exploratory nature and

Corporate Governance: Responsibilities, Risks and Remuneration. Edited by Kevin Keasey
and Mike Wright © 1997 John Wiley & Sons Ltd.

addresses several key areas, i.e. the extent to which institutional investors do use their voting rights, the issues which motivate them to do so, the mechanisms that exist for institutional investors to identify issues, and how institutional investors may reach a consensus on voting issues. The findings from the personal interviews carried out with institutional investors and their representative groups are analysed and salient features which emerge about the attitudes towards voting are highlighted. In addition, the extent to which institutional investors discharge their voting responsibilities is examined by an analysis of the voting levels in UK corporations.

The results of a survey on voting sent to the top 250 companies in the UK provide evidence of a low level of voting with, on average, only 35% of shares being voted. In 90% of the companies, the voting level is at 52% or less. These results have implications for UK institutional investors, who own between 65% and 75% of UK equity, and have been the object of criticism for not exercising their votes more. However, the detailed findings show that there is evidence that the larger institutional investors are voting to a greater extent than they were previously, but that other institutional investors are still not voting. The level of voting also appears to be dependent on the type of institutional investor (insurance company, pension fund, etc.).

A comparison is made with the USA, where institutional investors are also the predominant genre of investor. The internationalisation of institutional portfolios results in a cross-border interest in corporate governance which makes this a particularly interesting area to analyse. The US Department of Labor has stated clearly that it considers that the exercise of the vote is a fiduciary duty of shareholders, and it has expressed the view that US institutional shareholders should vote their stock both in the USA and overseas. The chapter concludes with recommendations designed to increase the level of voting in UK corporations.

INSTITUTIONAL INVESTMENT IN THE UK

The level of institutional investment in UK equities is significant, with the majority of shares held by insurance companies and pension funds. From Table 5.1 it can be seen that the total amount of institutional investment (measured by summary balance sheet values) in the UK rose from £569.4 billion in 1988 to £1073.0 billion in 1993, almost doubling in size over the six-year period. The split between investment trusts, unit trusts, long-

Table 5.1   Institutional Investment (Summary Balance Sheet Values)

	Investment trusts	Unit trusts	Long-term insurance companies	General insurance companies	Self administered pension funds	Total
			£ billion			
1988	20.3	41.1	200.2	40.0	267.8	569.4
1989	24.9	56.9	248.6	47.2	339.7	717.3
1990	20.6	46.1	234.0	42.7	303.1	646.5
1991	23.7	53.9	277.6	45.3	343.5	744.0
1992	29.9	63.1	328.4	51.7	382.2	855.1
1993	40.2	94.5	412.7	61.6	464.0	1073.0

Source: ABI Quarterly Statistics and Research Review, 1994.

term insurance companies, general insurance companies, and self-administered pension funds is also shown. Investment by long-term insurance companies grew from £200.2 billion to £412.7 billion, an increase of £212.5 billion (106%), while unit trusts' investment increased by 130% from £41.1 billion to £94.5 billion. Self-administered pension funds represent the largest sector of institutional investment, accounting for £464 billion of the total of £1073 billion invested (43%).

The insurance and pension fund institutional investors are represented by several bodies: the Association of British Insurers (ABI), NAPF, PIRC and the Institutional Fund Managers' Association (IFMA). Individual institutions will be swayed to some extent or other by the pronouncements of their representative bodies, although these are generally advisory in nature, usually taking the form of advocated best practice. All these main bodies have made statements detailing their views on institutional voting.

Recommendations by Institutional Bodies

The ABI represents over 450 insurance companies which between them account for over 90% of the business of UK insurance companies. The ABI recommends that large shareholders should vote wherever possible and support boards of directors unless they have good reason for doing otherwise. The rationale is that boards will become accustomed to receiving institutional support and will realise the severity of the situation if that support is not forthcoming on a particular issue.

The NAPF has over 1200 fund members and 350 other members, and is the UK's leading pension organisation. The NAPF recommends that its members have a voting policy and that they exercise their proxy votes whenever 'reasonably possible'. PIRC, on the other hand, is an independent consulting firm which provides advice on socially responsible investment and voting issues to institutional investors, mostly local government pension funds. PIRC recommends that 'shareholder voting rights should be exercised in an informed and independent manner'.

IFMA represents the interests of UK-based institutional fund managers and its membership accounts for well over 80% of total institutional funds managed in the UK. IFMA also advocates that votes should be exercised as frequently as possible, although they recognise that discretionary fund managers may face several difficulties in routinely exercising votes on behalf of clients. The most pertinent difficulty in this context is perhaps the administrative one of co-ordinating votes on behalf of large numbers of clients, particularly given that clients are prepared to delegate voting responsibility to differing degrees (i.e. fund manager may vote on all issues, on non-contentious issues only, or on no issues, without referring to the client). This is an issue that was cited by a number of respondents to the survey.

The ISC membership includes the ABI, Association of Investment Trust Companies (AITC), British Merchant Banking & Securities Houses Association, National Association of Pension Funds and the Association of Unit Trusts and Investment Funds. These institutions collectively represent 90% of institutional funds in the UK. In December 1991 the ISC issued *The Responsibilities of Institutional Investors in the UK*, in which it was advocated that institutions make positive use of their voting rights.

However, all the statements are recommendations: there are no explicit requirements to vote. Exercise of the vote is not a *requirement* of any of the institutional investor representative groups, neither is it one of the items listed in the Cadbury Committee's Code of Best Practice. However, the vote is a right attaching to share ownership, and many view it as a fundamental responsibility that this right is used to its best effect—that is, exercised in a considered way.

INSTITUTIONAL INVESTORS AND VOTING

The right to vote attached to an ordinary share is a fundamental aspect of share ownership and can be seen as a mechanism for ensuring that shareholders (the owners of the business) retain some control over management. The conflict between ownership and control is an inherent characteristic of the modern corporation and was identified as such by Berle and Means (1932) in their seminal work.

The high concentrations of institutional ownership of the shares of UK-quoted companies makes their relationships with the companies that they invest in quite different from that of a private shareholder with a company. However, as was pointed out in the Cadbury Report (1992),

'Institutional shareholders . . . are largely holding their shares on behalf of individuals, as members of pension funds, holders of insurance policies and the like. As a result, there is an important degree of common interest between individual and institutional shareholders. In particular both have the same stake in the standards of financial reporting and of governance in the companies in which they have invested' (paragraph 6.9).

The institutional investors, though, do have the all important ability, given their 'collective stake', to bring significant pressure to bear on companies, either by voting their shares or by informal discussion with management.

The context within which institutional investors might exercise their power can be thought of in terms of the 'exit and voice' framework developed by Hirschman (1970) in his seminal work. Hirschman argued that 'dissatisfaction [is expressed] directly to management or to some other authority to which management is subordinate or through general protest to anyone who cares to listen: this is the *voice* option' (p. 4). The alternative to this, the *exit* option, is not viable for many institutional investors as the size of their holdings and/or their policy of trying to hold a balanced portfolio makes selling their shares an unattractive option. The *voice* and *exit* options are however intertwined as 'the *effectiveness* of the voice mechanism is strengthened by the possibility of exit' (Hirschman, 1970, p. 83). According to Hirschman, it does not matter 'whether [the threat of exit] is made openly or whether the possibility of exit is merely well understood to be an element in the situation by all concerned' (p. 82).

Whittington (1993) recognises that

'Shareholders might incur very significant costs in exercising their monitoring function, particularly where shareholdings are diffuse. In order to influence the directors, the shareholders must combine with others to form a significant voting group which can pose a real threat of carrying resolutions or appointing directors at a general meeting. The costs of combining in this way might well be prohibitive relative to the benefits' (p. 313).

He suggests that one feasible approach that could be taken would be for large institutional investors to combine in some way to exert control by a block of voting power. This has significant implications for corporate governance and in the Greenbury Report (1995), one of the main action points is 'the investor institutions should use their power and influence to ensure the implementation of best practice as set out in the Code' (paragraph 3.4).

Although institutional investors are encouraged to exercise their votes, it is not clear that this is *necessarily* the rational thing for them to do, and whether one views the institutional investors attitude towards voting as rationality or complacency rather depends on (1) the perceived economic benefit of voting *per se*, (2) the size of the institutional holding, (3) the influence exercised by the institutional investor in any particular company and (4) the role of the institutional investor as a shareholder.

It could be argued that there is no economic benefit to voting: it may not matter which way they vote (or whether they vote at all) as the monetary differences of any particular course of action are not significant enough to go through the voting process. In other words, some institutional investors may feel that it is not worth expending any resources on voting since the marginal benefits are zero, or almost zero. This would apply both in cases of information asymmetry where the costs of making an informed decision outweigh the possible benefits, and also where a large number of beneficial shareholders would need to be contacted for their views (nominee shareholdings are a case in point). Some institutional investors may feel that their shareholdings are too small to have any real influence on a company, while at the other extreme, some institutional investors will exercise significant power behind the scenes. This influence has been described as the shareholder 'voice' (Hirschman, 1970; Black, 1990) and institutional investors may effect it through either formal or informal means.

From another viewpoint, the directors (managers) of the firm may view the presence of certain institutional investors as an implicit threat. The likely effect of this would be to make directors less willing to make decisions that would run counter to the perceived interests of this group. To the extent that the costs are borne by the directors, this could be construed as a bonding cost along the agency lines propounded by Jensen and Meckling (1976). This situation would mean that it was essentially unnecessary for institutional investors to vote as they would be exercising their power indirectly via their influence on the directors. It could also be argued that a characteristic of portfolio management is a passive shareholding but that company law assumes an individual active shareholding. This results in a mismatch between concepts of corporate governance, fiduciary duty and economic reality. However, as well as the fiduciary duty argument which has been strongly expressed in the USA, and is becoming increasingly so in the UK, studies on US data (Nesbitt, 1994; Gordon and Pound, 1993) have shown that in companies where institutional investors have taken a more active role in corporate governance issues (including voting) there is evidence of improved returns, i.e. an increase in shareholder wealth—a very real incentive for more active involvement.

The involvement of US institutional investors in US corporations is striking as they are active in voting and in putting forward anti-management proxy proposals (Thompson and Davis, 1992); in addition they vote, on average, 71% of their overseas proxies. The higher level of voting in the USA is partly attributable to the requirements of the Employee Retirement Income Security Act 1974 (ERISA), which established fiduciary standards for private pension funds. In this context the most pertinent point is that the voting of proxies in a considered manner, both in the USA and overseas, is viewed as a fiduciary responsibility of pension fund managers and trustees (see Mallin, 1995a, b, for a more detailed discussion of this). The influence of US institutions who invest in UK shares should not be underestimated. There has already been evidence of their influence with the withdrawal of a 'bundled' resolution by Hanson plc in 1993 which was heralded as 'one of the most successful public demonstrations of shareholder power ever seen in British corporate affairs' (*Guardian*, 19 June 1993). This resolution had aroused opposition, not only from UK investor groups but also from US funds, such as the State of Wisconsin Investment Board and the Florida State Board of Investment. Black and Coffee (1994) stated that

'As US institutions buy *and vote* more foreign shares, they appear to be inducing change in the traditional British practice of not bothering to vote. British institutions are finding that if they do not vote, foreign-held shares will carry disproportionate weight in the final tally' (p. 2084).

Brickley, Lease and Smith (1994) cite increasing institutional activism in the proxy process and highlight the fact that recent changes in SEC rules mean that institutional investors in the USA can more effectively form voting coalitions among investors. These recent changes mean that coalitions can more easily be formed by institutions without them being seen to be acting in concert.

Most institutional investors in the UK would assert that they do have a voting policy and that that policy is to vote their shares, although some have a policy of voting only on contentious issues. Broadly speaking, contentious issues are those which could be classed as non-routine. For example, a resolution which sought to reduce shareholders' rights would be viewed as contentious by most investors. A proposed takeover would be another example of a non-routine issue. Resolutions relating to executive remuneration, directors' share options and lengths of directors' service contracts have recently been the focus of attention. Among the institutional investors, groupings or forums are developing whereby institutional investors who wish to consult other institutions investing in a particular company have ready access to those institutions to discuss issues which they feel would benefit from such informal discussion. Such groupings add to the weight of the behind-the-scenes discussions which are a feature of the institutional investor–director relationship. Institutional investors already wield substantial power by virtue of their shareholdings, and together with their representative bodies are a powerful voice in the UK voting arena. The exercise of their votes is viewed by most institutions as a fundamental responsibility: behind-the-scenes discussion may achieve much, but the exercise of the vote is both a show of support for management and a powerful deterrent against errant or misguided management who try to act in ways that may not be in shareholders' best interests.

PREVIOUS VOTING RESEARCH

There has been a lack of academic research into voting levels in the UK. Research in this area has tended to be confined to that carried out by the representative institutional bodies such as the National Association of Pension Funds (NAPF), Institutional Shareholders' Committee (ISC), Pensions Investment Research Consultants Limited (PIRC), and ProShare. These studies are discussed below.

NAPF Studies

The NAPF has undertaken an annual survey of occupational pensions since 1975. Part of the survey looks at *voting intent*, and asks respondents to categorise their voting intent as: 'Vote at all times if practicable', 'not vote', 'vote only on contentious issues', or 'other'.

The 1990 survey (results relate to 1989) indicated that 20% of UK pension funds had the intention of regularly exercising their voting rights. The latest survey undertaken in 1993 shows that this percentage had increased to 26%. While the overall level of intent to vote at all times is still low at 26%, it does represent a 30% increase on the 1990 survey figure. It should also be noted that the 1993 survey covered 615 private sector pension funds and 51 public sector funds (total 666), whereas the 1990 survey covered a smaller number of pension funds: 492 private sector, 46 public sector (total 538). A larger number of smaller schemes are now filling in the survey, and NAPF have stated that, overall, the results would seem to indicate that not only has the level of intent to vote on all issues increased but the larger number of respondents includes many smaller pension funds which would also appear to try to vote at all times if practicable.

ISC Study

The ISC carried out a survey into the use of voting rights in 1993. Twenty companies reported on the extent to which each of the 20 largest institutional shareholdings in their companies were voted. These shareholdings amounted, on average, to 30% of the equity. The ISC found that, on average, 70% of the insurance-related holdings were voted compared with 44% of the pension-related holdings. The latter figure is a substantial increase on the findings of the NAPF survey discussed above, which showed that only approximately 26% of pension funds would vote. However, the ISC survey dealt only with the largest holdings, which would probably tend to be characterised by a higher voting level than pension funds generally.

The ISC found that, in the twenty companies researched, an average 34% of all shares were voted. This was a substantial increase on an earlier study carried out by the ISC in 1990, which showed that the average voting level was 20%. An important result was the substantial difference between the level of voting of insurance-related holdings compared to pension-related holdings.

PIRC Study

PIRC carried out a survey in 1993 of FTSE 100 companies, asking for figures for proxy votes cast. Approximately one third of companies supplied the figures requested. The PIRC study found that, on average, only 9% of registered shareholders returned proxy forms, although these did account for an average 33% of shares in issue. This is indicative of proxy voting being more prevalent among larger institutional investors. Despite the reported low level of 9%, many companies did report an increase in the number of proxy votes received. PIRC report that the largest increase of shares voted was from 25% to 46.5%, and that the lowest figure for proxies lodged covered only 11% of shares.

It was also pointed out that some companies make their proxy voting figures available as a matter of course. Examples include Fisons, which made these figures available at the registration desk at its AGM, and Scottish Power, which announced the figures before every resolution at its AGM.

ProShare Study

ProShare represents the interests of individual investors rather than institutional investors. However, ProShare's survey on proxy cards, sent out to its members, reports some interesting findings. ProShare was told by company registrars that only between 9% and 12% of proxies were generally returned. However, in the ProShare Survey, 24% (226 members) stated that they always returned proxy forms, while a further 34% (325 members) stated that they usually did so. ProShare states that their members are probably 'more inclined to vote than shareholders in total, but that many feel that it is not worthwhile because of their small holdings'.

Summary of Findings to Date

The surveys to date have shown that the overall level of voting is quite low. Institutional investors in the insurance industry would appear to be the most active in voting. There does, however, appear to be a 'trickle' effect as more proxies are being returned, and the level of voting of, for example, pension funds has increased over the last three or four years. In general, though, the increases are from a small base. It would require substantial increases to reflect a *real* change in attitude towards voting.

The studies discussed above are each subject to various limitations: the NAPF survey is sent only to pension funds, the ISC and PIRC survey results were based on a small number of respondents, and the ProShare survey was of individual, rather than institutional, shareholders. In this chapter the limitations in the studies discussed above are addressed. The following two sections analyse (1) institutional investors' views towards voting, based on face-to-face interviews with a range of institutional investors, and (2) the voting levels in UK corporations, based on a questionnaire sent to the Top 250. In addition, from the questionnaire responses, the views of company secretaries on the voting process are also analysed.

INSTITUTIONAL INVESTORS INTERVIEWS

Corporate governance is a dynamic and evolving area. The Cadbury Report (1992) states that 'we look to the institutions in particular . . . to use their influence as owners to ensure that the companies in which they have invested comply with the Code' (paragraph 6.16). The Cadbury Committee also 'warmly welcomed' the ISC recommendation that 'institutional investors should make positive use of their voting rights, unless they have good reason for doing otherwise. They should register their votes wherever possible on a regular basis' (paragraph 6.11). Given this emphasis on the role of institutional investors in the UK corporate governance arena, and the lack of published research in this field, it was felt that interviews with institutional investors and their representative groups to elicit their views would provide important new evidence.

Accordingly, 28 interviews were carried out with various institutional investors and their representative groups to ascertain their views on voting and the role of institutional investors in corporate governance. Those interviewed encompassed investment management companies (including pension funds, insurance companies and multi-client investment managers), the Association of British Insurers, the National Association of Pension Funds, Pensions Investment Research Consultants, Association of Investment Trust Companies, Institutional Fund Managers' Association, Institutional Shareholders Committee, Institute of Directors, the London Stock Exchange and Sir Adrian Cadbury. This range of senior level interviewees provided a rich source of opinion in the face-to-face interviews. Most interviews lasted an hour or slightly longer and focused on the voting policies of institutional investors and their involvement in corporate governance issues. The views that emerged from these interviews are discussed below.

Most of the institutional investors interviewed stated that they had a policy of voting their shares on all resolutions. For some the voting policy covered all of their shareholdings, while for others all holdings representing over 1% of the company. For the latter group, the intention seems to be that eventually all shareholdings would be voted. A small minority expressed a policy of voting only on contentious or non-routine issues on the basis that voting as a matter of course could reduce voting to a 'box-ticking' exercise without due consideration being given to the issues being voted on. The counter-argument to this is that institutional investors who vote regularly, and then choose not to vote on a particular issue, will find that their action makes more of an impression on the company.

It was also felt that the informal meetings and discussions with company management provided a forum in which the institutional investors could make their views known, and where any differences of opinion could be resolved without the added pressures of public involvement. This kind of informal discussion should mean that there is less chance of the share price being affected by the company being a focus of unwelcome media attention. The dialogue with management is seen as central to the management/institutional investor relationship and where management is actively involved in dialogue with its institutional investors, then it can normally be expected that its institutional investors will be supportive of incumbent management.

The interviewees tended to follow a similar approach in their assessment of the resolutions on a company's AGM (or other general meeting) agenda. Initially the company's annual report and accounts would be reviewed, together with the notice of resolutions to be voted on at the forthcoming meeting. The resolutions would be examined to see if any resolution represented a possible conflict with either the institutional investor's own guidelines or with those of a particular client. Most of the institutional investors receive at least one of the voting services provided by the ABI, NAPF, or PIRC, and review the comments made by each service on a particular company's resolutions. When an institutional investor notices a resolution which they feel falls within their definition of contentious, or non-routine, then dialogues may occur in one or more of several directions, i.e. (1) contacting other institutional investors with interests in the company (disclosable shareholdings are readily available, and in any case, many institutional investors will be aware of the other large institutional shareholdings in various companies); (2) contacting the relevant institutional investor representative group(s); and (3) contacting the company to express their concern at that particular resolution. These modes of dialogue epitomise the view expressed by Hirschman (1970) 'for voice to function properly it is necessary that individuals possess reserves of political influence which they can bring into play when they are sufficiently aroused' (p. 71). A few institutions are generally perceived as 'vanguard' institutions who are particularly active in encouraging corporate governance best practice: institutions such as the Prudential, Standard Life and Postel.

Coalitions of institutional shareholders tend to be formed if there is some sort of crisis. For example, a company might be seriously under-performing with the result that the share price is deteriorating; or there might be a dominant chairman/CEO who could threaten the institutional investment in the company by his or her actions. Generally, one or more of the large institutional investors will take the lead and 'mobilise' other institutional investors to join the coalition. Smaller institutional investors may choose to sell their shareholding (the exit alternative) but larger ones would find this a less attractive strategy as the share price would tend to fall as larger holdings come onto the market. On occasion the action can be co-ordinated through a representative body, such as the ABI, and the cost of the action is then spread among that organisation's members, thus reducing any free-rider problem. Generally, the coalitions of institutional investors succeed in their behind-the-scenes discussions with manage-ment, and very few disputes come to a vote where the institutional investors would be making public their opposition to a particular resolu-tion. However, there have been a few isolated occurrences of a more public approach, for example the struggle by a coalition of institutional investors to replace the board of Tace which took place in 1991. This episode highlighted very real difficulties of keeping together a coalition of institutional investors, and the eventual victory left the two lead institutions with a large legal bill to which other institutions declined to contribute. This public approach is also anathema to the traditional British 'softly, softly' attitude and tends to be used only as a measure of last resort.

Most company resolutions are routine in nature and so would not prove contentious. Such routine resolutions include: approving the annual report and accounts; (re)appointment of auditors; approving the auditors' fees; and approving the dividend for the year. Other company resolutions may be more contentious and Table 5.2 is a taxonomy of voting intent on contentious, or non-routine, issues and illustrates the way that institutional investors would tend to vote on certain issues, although the classifications are 'broad brush' and give an indication of the way that votes would *generally* be cast.

Once a decision to vote a particular way has been reached (with reference back to specific clients for guidance if they so request) then the

Table 5.2   Taxonomy of Voting Intent by Type of Resolution

Type of resolution Voting	Intent
Disapplication of pre-emption rights beyond 10% of issued share capital	Against
Reduction in shareholder rights	Against
Appointment of directors on contracts longer than 2 years	Against
Appointment of one director to the posts of chairman and CEO	Against
Appointment of directors on rolling three-year contracts	Against
Appointment of directors aged 70 years or over	Against
Any resolution not complying with the Cadbury Code	Against
Executive share options not linked to performance measures	Against
Non-executive directors in post for more than 10 years	Against
Ex-gratia payments to retiring directors	Against

votes are cast. Votes should be maintained in a voting log, with any abstentions or 'against' votes recorded. Some institutions do carry out *ex-post* analysis of voting to ensure that (1) the vote has been cast and (2) it has been cast correctly, but this is by no means universal practice.

To summarise, most institutional investors stated that they try to vote on all issues wherever possible, and, as one interviewee stated, 'with managing funds on behalf of other people goes the responsibility to exercise the votes'. A minority of institutional investors vote only on contentious issues, on the basis that to vote on all issues, routine and non-routine, becomes a box-ticking exercise, performed without due consideration of the issues at hand. Given that the majority of institutional investors do seem to have a policy of voting, it was decided to send a survey on voting to the Top 250 companies in the UK to determine what levels of voting they were actually experiencing.

SURVEY RESULTS

A survey of voting patterns was sent to the Company Secretary of each of the Top 250 companies (by turnover) in the UK, with data being obtained from Datastream. Company Secretaries tend to be involved in the corporate governance function in their companies and are usually the respondents to questionnaires in the corporate governance area (see, for example, Conyon, 1995). It was felt that Company Secretaries would be in a good position to be aware of the level of voting in their company, and of issues related to voting. The survey was designed to elicit the latter information as well as their views on the wider aspects of corporate governance. The survey adopted an open-ended approach given the exploratory nature of the research. There were 101 completed surveys returned, with respondents being reasonably spread across the Top 250. In addition, some 45 respondents returned surveys stating that they were unable to complete the survey for several reasons: mainly time pressures, lack of available information, or that it was company policy not to complete surveys. The responses were analysed using SPSS.

The responses related to Annual General Meetings (AGMs) over the period November 1993 to September 1994, which covered accounting periods ending from June 1993 to May 1994. The most popular time for an AGM seems to be May (31%), followed by July (22%), then April (16%). As one might expect, the most common accounting year ends are December and March, the former being the calendar year end and the latter having historical connections with the fiscal year end for income tax (which affected companies prior to the introduction of corporation tax).

Level of Voting

The level of voting is illustrated in Figure 5.1. The level of voting is clearly not as high as might be expected given the level of institutional

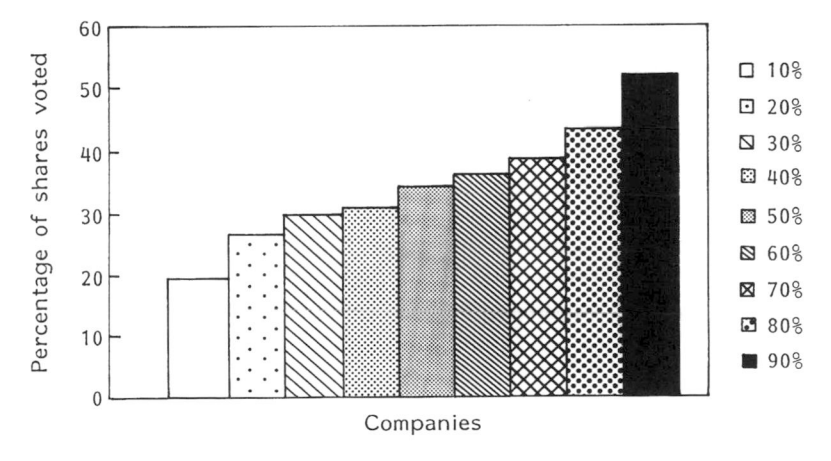

Figure 5.1   Percentage of Shares Voted at Last AGM

ownership and the assertion by most institutions that they do exercise their votes. The mean level of voting is about 35%. As regards the breakdown of voting for the last AGM, in 50% of companies, the level of voting is 34% or less, while 10% of companies experience a voting level of less than 20%. Ninety per cent of respondent companies experience a voting level of 52% or less. From some points of view, this would seem to be a reasonable level of voting given various perceived administrative problems (discussed further below) in the voting process. It should also be remembered that many institutions will make their views known in behind-the-scenes discussions with management. It is possible that some of these institutions may not then vote on issues, their 'silence' indicating approval (or disapproval if the discussions were not fruitful).

Disclosable Interests

Substantial shareholdings of 3% or more have to be disclosed in the company's annual report, and most companies have tended to make this disclosure in the directors' report. There were 225 individual disclosable interests reported from all the respondent companies which had disclosable interests (88%). Fifty per cent of the respondent companies had disclosable interests totalling 13.5% or less. The mean disclosable interest was about 18.5% (partly attributable to some quite substantial disclosable interests for some companies). A holding of 3% or more in a company in the Top 250 is likely to represent a substantial financial investment.

It might have been thought that there would be a positive relationship between the proportion of shares held in a company and the propensity to vote those shares. The results in total do not indicate this. However, if the individual institutional investors are examined in more detail, it can be seen that there is a relationship between the voting level and the proportion of shares held, *where those shares are held by particular institutions*. Taking the Prudential as an example, the Prudential has a 3% disclosable interest in twelve respondent companies, 4% in seven, 5% in ten, 6% in three, 7% in four, 11% in one and 13% in one. How, then, does the level of voting in these companies in which the Prudential does have a disclosable interest compare to those companies in which it does not?

In Table 5.3 the total levels of voting are compared with the Prudential's level of disclosable interest in companies. There seems to be evidence of a trend whereby as the level of voting increases, so does the proportion of companies in which the Prudential has disclosable interests. For example, at the point where the level of voting is at 20% or less, the Prudential has

Table 5.3 Prudential's Disclosable Interests and Total Voting Levels (%)

Company's total voting level	Proportion of companies invested in by Prudential	Proportion of Prudential's disclosable interests
Less than 20	20.0	5.6
20–30	16.7	8.3
30–35	50.0	25.0
35–40	50.0	27.8
40–50	50.0	16.7
50+	54.5	16.7

disclosable interests in only 20% of those companies, whereas when the level of voting is at 50% or more, the Prudential has disclosable interests in 55%. Of Prudential's total disclosable interests (in the respondent companies), only 5.6% are in the companies with the lowest level of voting, while the largest proportion of Prudential's disclosable interests (28%) are in companies with a voting level of 35–40%. The companies with the highest level of voting of 50% or more account for nearly 17% of Prudential's disclosable interests. It was also found that Standard Life, which had disclosable interests in 11% of the companies, tended to have its largest proportion of disclosable interests (44%) concentrated in those companies with voting levels of 35% or more, while 33% of its disclosable interests are in companies with voting levels of 50% or more.

There does therefore seem to be some evidence that the presence of certain institutional investors may be connected with increased voting levels in the companies in which they have disclosable interests. It may be that these companies attract the large institutional investors and it is worth the large institutional investors incurring the research costs associated with informed voting. It is possible that a large institutional investor may incur the search costs and other institutional investors will then vote in the same way: this idea of collusive voting was discussed above.

Voting Levels of the Twenty Largest Institutional Investors

The voting levels of the twenty largest institutional investors in each company were analysed by the type of institution, using the information supplied by respondents in Table A of the survey (37 respondents completed Table A). Table 5.4 shows the level of voting of the respondent companies' twenty largest institutional investors, split into the main types

Table 5.4 Summary of Voting by Companies' Twenty Largest Institutional Investors (%)

Insurance companies	Pension funds	Unit trusts	Investment trusts	Nominees	Total voting by top 20 institutional investors	Total voting by all investors
77.6	72.4	72.3	53.4	37.1	57.1	34.95

of institutional investor: insurance companies, pension funds, unit trusts, investment trusts and nominee holdings. The last two columns show the total level of voting across the respondent companies by the twenty largest institutional investors and the level of voting by all investors (private and institutional).

Of particular note is the fact that the voting levels of both the insurance- and pension-related groups were fairly high, with the institutional investors from the insurance industry voting, on average, 77.6% of their shares, and the institutional investors from the pensions industry voting, on average, 72.4% of their shares. As might have been expected, given the perceived administrative difficulties of voting nominee holdings, the level of voting for nominee holdings averages 37.1%, the lowest level of the largest twenty institutional investors groupings.

The findings are particularly encouraging for the pension funds when compared with the ISC 1993 survey finding (looking at the twenty largest institutional investors in twenty large companies) that 43.7% of pension-related holdings were voted. The trend is also upwards for the insurance industry with an increase from 70.2% found by the ISC in 1993 to 77.6%.

Two inferences can be made at this stage. First, the average level of voting by the twenty largest institutional investors in the respondent companies is 57.1%, which is substantially more than the average level of voting by *all* investors in these companies (34.95%). Second, given the high level of institutional ownership in the UK, there must be a significant number of institutional investors who do not constitute the twenty largest shareholders, who either have a low level of voting or do not vote at all.

Further analysis found that in 27% of companies the insurance funds and pension funds have equal levels of voting, in 21% of companies the pension funds have higher levels of voting than the insurance funds, and that in 52% of companies the insurance funds have higher levels of voting than the pension funds. In 81% of companies the voting level of the twenty largest institutional investors was greater than the average level of voting in the company overall, while in 19% of companies the level of voting of the twenty largest institutional investors was less than the average level of voting in the company overall. This latter finding may be attributable to problems with nominee accounts, and perhaps some management houses have decided that it is too expensive to organise the votes on all the smaller holdings under their control. Some management houses have 160–200 different client funds and with the cost of a proxy being approximately £60–80 a time, then they may view the costs as too burdensome.

The Voting Process

A number of comments were made by respondents about the voting process. While 19% of comments stated that the voting process was straightforward and that there were no problems with it, this was not the view of the majority. The most significant factor cited was possible difficulties associated with nominee holdings, and the problems in identifying the beneficial owners of the shares, and obtaining their views on how they would wish to vote on any particular issue (50%). The present situation is rather cumbersome, and may result in the beneficial owners being disenfranchised due to timing delays. This is obviously a particular problem where the beneficial owners are overseas.

Some 13% of the responses were quite critical of institutional investors, stating that it was 'very difficult' to get proxy forms from the institutions. Indeed, there is anecdotal evidence of companies which have a campaign in a particular year, chasing every institutional investor owning more than a certain percentage of shares and trying to persuade them to vote their shares. The problem is that while the voting level may go up in the year of the campaign, it falls back to a lower level in the following year!

Voting Behaviour of Institutional and Private Investors

Respondents were asked for their views on the main differences between the voting behaviour of institutional investors and the voting behaviour of private investors. Some respondents took the view that there were no discernible differences in the voting behaviour of the two groups (14%). However, the majority of responses did cite differences between the two groups. The main differences were that there was less consensus from individual investors and that they sometimes appeared to vote in an

arbitrary or irrational manner (13%), and 3% thought that private investors might not understand some resolutions and were more likely to vote
against complex or technical issues. A further 16% of respondents stated
that private (individual) investors often seemed more emotional about
certain issues, particularly directors' salaries and option schemes, and
directors' appointments. The specific issues cited (directors' salaries, etc.)
are ones which are also of key importance to institutional investors,
although institutions were thought to be generally supportive (11%) and
contentious issues would often be the subject of the behind-the-scenes
discussions explicitly mentioned by 10% of respondents.

Voting Behaviour of Different Types of Institutional Investor

It was thought that there might be differences in the voting behaviour of
various types of institutional investor (pension funds, insurance companies, etc.). While 44% of responses felt that there were either no
differences or no discernible differences, 8% felt that certain pension
funds and, on occasion, US institutions tended to take a stance on certain
issues. Four per cent felt that insurance companies were more inclined to
vote and 5% felt that both insurance companies and pension funds were
voting, and that institutional voting was on the increase. Eight per cent
felt that there were problems in voting for nominee holdings representing
large mixes of shareholders, and for unit trusts and investment trusts.
Possible problems in relation to nominee holdings have been discussed
above. Mention was made of the institutional investors' representative
bodies, with 10% expressing the view that the voting behaviour of an
institution was dependent on the views of its 'mouthpiece' institution.

Main Criteria for Effective Corporate Governance

Many respondents cited the fact that they approved of, and followed, the
Cadbury Code (16%). Others mentioned specific individual criteria that
they perceived as important for effective corporate governance. These
were strong independent non-executive directors (19%), division of the
roles of Chairman and CEO (13%), audit committees (13%) and remuneration committees (5%). Another 13% of responses emphasised the
importance of regular, efficiently run board meetings, with written
responsibilities for the board, involvement of the *full* board with all
strategy and investment decisions, and clearly defined levels of authority.
Other criteria mentioned included those embodied in the Cadbury Code,

plus the importance of a compliance/company
adequate company wide authority to ensure
pliance.

Areas of Possible Disagreement with the Cadbury

Most respondents indicated general support for most
Code, and in many cases felt that it fitted with the ◡xisting
governance procedures. The main comments were a ◡ught have been
expected, with 17% feeling that there were difficulties with internal
control/going-concern reporting and 12% feeling that the Cadbury Code
was overly prescriptive for small companies. These two comments are
fairly indicative of any criticisms that have been made of the Cadbury
Code.

Other comments made were that the role of non-executive directors
tended to be overemphasised, the two-tier board possibility should have
been more closely looked at, and that care should be taken that there is
not too much bureaucracy, which could interfere with a company's ability
to pursue its objectives.

POLICY RECOMMENDATIONS

The responses to this questionnaire have shown that there is a keen
interest in corporate governance, and in voting patterns. However, from
the responses, the voting levels in the Top 250 companies in the UK have
been shown to average about 35%, with some companies considerably
below this level, while 90% of respondent companies have a voting level
of 52% or less. Many would consider that these levels of voting are far
too low, and would advocate measures to improve the level of voting.
Others would argue that there are complex administrative procedures to
take into consideration, particularly with nominee holdings and the
problems of ascertaining the wishes of beneficial owners with regard to
voting on various issues.

The detailed analysis has shown that the twenty largest institutional
investors in each company exhibit voting levels of 77.6% and 72.4%,
respectively, for the insurance- and pension-related holdings. The much
lower average for the total voting level (35%) reflects the fact that many
institutional investors who do not fall within the group of the twenty
largest investors would not appear to exercise their votes.

ing that an active involvement in effective voting (i.e. know-
able or informed voting) is to be encouraged, it is recommended that
the following measures be considered as possible means of increasing the
voting levels in the UK:

1. *Companies to disclose in a published form the **level of voting** on each
   resolution at the last AGM* This would serve to highlight both overall
   voting levels and specific issues which had attracted the highest level
   of voting interest. This published information could be released at the
   same time as other company information, for example interim results,
   which would help to contain costs. Corporations in the USA have to
   disclose this information and it would be informative for shareholders
   and other interested parties if this were also disclosed in the UK.
2. *Institutional investors to disclose both their voting policy (for example,
   to vote on all issues) and the level of voting that they have achieved
   in the companies in which they invest* This could probably take the
   form of disclosure in terms of bands of voting, for example 'in 75%
   of the companies we invest in, we voted 80% of the shares'. This
   information would be useful to many parties interested in shareholders
   visibly playing an active role, and would make transparent the institutional investors' voting policies.
3. *Ex-post analysis of their voting by institutions* Institutions could carry
   out an analysis of how they had voted to ensure that voting was in
   accordance with their voting policy statement, and was actually taking
   place. *Ex-post* analysis would, in any case, be necessary if institutions
   were to disclose the suggested information about their level of voting.
4. *Industry standard clause in clients' contracts giving fund managers the
   discretion to vote the shares in accordance with their detailed voting
   policy statement* The client would generally agree to this clause, or if
   they wanted to retain discretion, then an additional administration fee
   would be charged to cover the extra work involved in referring back to
   the individual client for specific voting instructions. This would help to
   alleviate some of the problems of nominee accounts, and where
   management funds manage hundreds of smaller clients.
5. *A guide to proxy voting could be disseminated to all investors* This
   would be of particular interest to private investors, although it would
   prove useful to some institutions as well.
6. *Streamlining of the proxy voting procedures in all institutions* This
   would ensure that institutional investors would be able to vote proxies
   in a timely way.
7. *Companies should be informed in good time of the person responsible
   for completing proxy forms* This would have a twofold purpose, first,
   to ensure that institutions themselves identify who is responsible, and
   second, companies would know exactly who to chase for proxies.

Hopefully, the two combined would mean that proxies would be received by companies on a more timely basis.

8. *It is helpful if companies have a strong secretariat function* A strong, efficient secretariat could advise on corporate governance matters generally, and act as a monitoring function, including chasing proxies.

CONCLUSIONS

The measures outlined above could help to raise the level and effectiveness of voting. As discussed, there have been some encouraging signs, with some institutions actively pursuing a policy of voting all their shares wherever possible, but the level of voting overall is still low. The institutional investors in the UK need to recognise the growing influence of US institutional investors in overseas markets, especially with the clarification of the ERISA requirements by the US Department of Labor (1994), which declared that the voting of foreign proxies would generally be viewed in the same way as it views domestic proxies, i.e. overseas proxies should be voted wherever possible. Institutional Shareholder Services in the USA stated in 1994 'regardless of the actual size of US holdings, proxy voting activities by US institutional shareholders in global markets has helped bring many corporate governance issues out into the open in several countries, sparking domestic activity and influencing existing debates in these countries'. It is clear that US institutional investors are looking to extend their corporate governance policies/influences to overseas countries. US institutional investors tend to be more proactive than their UK counterparts, as epitomised by the higher voting levels of 60–80% or more. There have already been instances in UK companies of US investors votes cast outnumbering those of UK investors votes cast (for example, Saatchi and Saatchi), even though the US shareholdings were less than those held by UK investors. The internationalisation of institutional portfolios and the resulting cross-border interest in corporate governance mean that UK investors must now vote their shares in much larger numbers. It is no longer acceptable for institutional investors to take a complacent attitude to voting or to rationalise not voting on the basis of incomplete or inaccurate perceptions of the importance of voting. Inherent in this new commitment would be the acceptance of voting as a part of the prudent investment principle, and the acceptance that voting is a fundamental aspect of fiduciary duty.

REFERENCES

Berle, A.A. and Means, G.C. (1932) *The Modern Corporation and Private Property*, New York: Macmillan.

Black, B.S. (1990) Shareholder passivity reexamined. *Michigan Law Review*, **89**, No. 3, 520–608.

Black, B.S. and Coffee, J.C. (1994) Hail Britannia? Institutional investor behaviour under limited regulation. *Michigan Law Review*, **92**, No. 7, 1997–2087.

Brickley, J.A., Lease, R.C. and Smith, C.W. (1994) Corporate voting: evidence from charter amendment proposals. *Journal of Corporate Finance*, **1**, No. 1, March, 5–31.

Cadbury Committee (1992) *Report on Committee on the Financial Aspects of Corporate Governance*, London: Gee & Co.

Central Statistical Office (CSO) (1994) *Share Ownership: The Share Register Survey Report end 1993*, London: HMSO.

Conyon, M. (1995) Institutional arrangements for setting directors' compensation in UK companies. Warwick Business School mimeo.

Gordon, L. and Pound, J. (1993) *Report to the California Public Employees' Retirement System: Active Investing in the U.S. Equity Market: Past Performance and Future Prospects*, Newton, MA: Gordon Group Inc.

Greenbury Report (1995) *Directors' Remuneration—Report of a Study Group Chaired by Sir Richard Greenbury*, London: Gee & Co.

Hirschman, A. (1970) *Exit, Voice, and Loyalty: Responses to Decline in Firms, Organizations, and States*, Cambridge, MA: Harvard University Press, September.

Institutional Shareholders' Committee (ISC) (1991) *The Responsibilities of Institutional Shareholders in the U.K.*, London.

Institutional Shareholders' Committee (ISC) (1993) *Report on Investigation of Use of Voting Rights By Institutions*, London.

Jensen, M.C. and Meckling, W.H. (1976) Theory of the firm: managerial behaviour, agency costs and ownership structure. *Journal of Financial Economics*, **3**, 305–60.

Mallin, C.A. (1995a) *Voting: The Role of Institutional Investors in Corporate Governance*, London: The Institute of Chartered Accountants in England and Wales.

Mallin, C.A. (1995b) The voting framework: a comparative study of voting by institutional investors in the U.S. and the U.K. Warwick Business School mimeo.

National Association of Pension Funds (NAPF) (1993) *Annual Survey of Occupational Pensions*, London.

Nesbitt, S.L. (1994) *Long-Term Rewards From Corporate Governance*, Santa Monica, CA: Wilshire Associates Incorporated.

Pensions Investment Research Consultants (PIRC) Limited (1993) Do proxies count? PIRC surveys FTSE 100. *PIRC Intelligence*, **7**, Issue 6, July/August.

Proshare (1994) Proxy cards. *Proshare Survey*, May.

Thompson, T. and Davis, G.F. (1992) Collective action and the battle for corporate control: institutional investors as a social movement. *Academy of Management Best Papers Proceedings*.

US Department of Labor (1994) Secretary Reich advocates corporate activist role for pension plans. *News Bulletin*, 28 July.

Whittington, G. (1993) Corporate governance and the regulation of financial reporting. *Accounting and Business Research*, **23**, No. 91A, 311–19.

Index